ALSO BY DAVID BELSON

Tributes and Forms for Public Occasions

Speeches for Every Occasion (with Ruth Belson)

What to Say *for* Every Occasion

MODEL SPEECHES,
LETTERS, AND REMARKS

∾

DAVID BELSON

BARNES
&NOBLE
BOOKS
NEW YORK

Published by MJF Books
Fine Communications
322 Eighth Avenue
New York, NY 10001

What to Say for Every Occasion
LC Control Number 2002106261
ISBN 1-56731-541-0

Manufactured in the United States of America on acid-free paper ∞

MJF Books and the MJF colophon are trademarks of Fine Creative
Media, Inc.

QM   10 9   8   7   6   5   4   3

TO MY WIFE, RUTH

Contents

Introduction

Nearly everyone is called upon, at some time or another, to prepare a speech or compose other material to be spoken, read or used in his club, school, community center, religious or other group activity. Incidental to these activities, meetings are conducted; speeches are delivered for various purposes and causes; officers are installed; gifts are presented and accepted; testimonials are tendered to deserving persons; resolutions, scrolls and written documents and data of all kinds are drafted.

Many would like to become active in their community, welfare, fraternal and other endeavors. They would like to exercise their rights and perform their obligations as members of their community. But they are deterred from so doing because they either lack sufficient time to compose and organize the material which is required of them, or they cannot locate a satisfactory source of material; possibly they do not have the essential training to perform the obligations of such group activities.

It is for those who are painfully groping their way

and struggling with the difficulties of composition that this work holds out a helping hand.

To draft a resolution or compose a speech is an art and demands the exercise of skill. Every workman in the exercise of his art should be provided with proper implements. The author and public speaker employ for the accomplishment of their purposes, the dictionary, the thesaurus, and reference books. The lawyer has his form books without which he would be greatly handicapped. While there is no dearth of books on public speaking, there is an absence of books devoted primarily to furnishing materials, illustrations and guides. This work gives a generous amount of such data. It is long on illustration and short on explanation which is the function of the books on public speaking.

It is hoped that the character and variety of forms and illustrations will enable the user adequately to cope with the usual situations with which he may be confronted. The material furnished will often answer the queries, "What shall I say?" "How shall I say it?" and save anxious hours of composing. The user can readily select out of the collection of material and illustrations those expressions and examples which are best suited for his purpose. The models should be modified and conformed to the user's personality and his special needs. Most of these forms, which have been shorn of excess verbiage, have been used and tested in the public arena. Many of the forms may be adapted or used for written statements or letters.

To save space no attention has been given to paragraphing the illustrations. When models are used in letter writing they require, of course, a proper salutation such as, "Dear Friend," or "Dear Sir," and a closing as, for instance, "Fraternally yours," "Sincerely yours," or other appropriate closing.

Grateful acknowledgment is made to the following organizations whose convention and annual meeting reports and other published material have supplied the basis for some of the illustrations used:

> American Federation of Labor
>
> Amalgamated Meat Cutters and
> Butcher Workmen of North America
>
> The Commission on American Citizenship
> of the Catholic University of America.

DAVID BELSON

What to Say *for* Every Occasion

1. Presentations

Here is a speech situation that could confront you on very short notice. The occasion often arises that an officer of your lodge, for example, is retiring and it has been suggested that a gift be presented. You have been selected to make the presentation address. There are two steps in the formulation of the speech of presentation: (1) praise the recipient, and (2) tender the gift.

To aid in preparing the talk, material and complete examples to meet the usual situation are given in this chapter.

Following these examples of the breakdown of the speech of presentation into its two component parts are completed illustrations combining step one and step two, constituting the entire speech of presentation. In every chapter of this book, whenever a formula is provided for organizing a speech, examples of each step will be given, followed by completed illustrations.

Decide which of the illustrations most clearly approaches the requirements of your own assignment. Then adapt it to your special needs.

1. Praise for recipient

You have shown yourself to be a man of courage, humility and integrity as well as great personal charm. Your outstanding contributions to interracial and inter-faith movements mark you as a true American in the best traditions of our democracy. To me, you represent the embodiment of what is good, fine, righteous and admirable.

◆

Your deeds speak for you far better than anything I can say. You have devoted yourself unselfishly to a host of humanitarian causes. Your activities have been so extensive it would almost seem one lifetime could not encompass them all. Yet you have found the time and the energy to serve, to work and to lead, shouldering countless burdens with unfailing good humor and grace.

◆

Your many activities have brought you richly deserved honors in the past.

◆

You have been a tower of strength and a strong force for progressive, efficient public service.

◆

In all of our dealings with you, you have always shown patience and tolerance—qualities which you are going to need as president of this great organization.

◆

In the course of your duties, you have earned the respect of all members and officers of our organization for your integrity and sincerity. Your neighbors in the community in which you live have recognized your worth by electing you president of the P.T.A.

◆

You have advanced through every rank. You combine tenacity with dynamic action. You have the reputation of being incorruptible. Your knowledge of the men you worked with and their faith in you has helped to restore public confidence in the force. The community is grateful to you for the public service you have performed.

◆

You are a vital and effective force in the great growth of this Association. To the presidents who came and went, you have been a guide and counselor; to our treasurer, you have been a big brother and helpful associate; to the directors, the chairman and members of our many committees, you have been the aid and mentor; and to our staff, you have been the understanding and directing father. To all of us, you have given your heart and you received in return our boundless admiration and affection.

◆

I am very sorry from a selfish point of view to see Mr. Doe retire. I have depended upon him to so great an extent that I am going to miss him deeply.

◆

You have long been a figure in the public life. You have always taken a keen interest in amateur sports. You are active in fraternal matters and have been honored by the Grand Order. You have merited the commendation of your fellow citizens.

2. Tender of the Gift or Award

Please accept this gift as an expression of our sincere gratitude for all you have done to further the work of our organization. It is our fervent hope that you may long enjoy your new-found leisure.

✦

I have a very pleasant duty to perform and that is to make formal presentation to you of the emblem of your office. I know it will represent for you the fruits of many years of service to this organization. I present this gavel and with it go our best wishes for a successful administration.

✦

We dedicate this plaque as a reminder that these honored dead, through their vigorous and active devotion to American ideals and the American way of life, have set a standard for us to emulate.

✦

I present this to you as a token of my warm affection and esteem and as a remembrance of what has been for me, at least, a uniquely happy relationship. May you find satisfaction and fulfillment in your new position and may you enjoy happiness and good health for many years to come!

✦

I am happy for this opportunity to add my expression of gratitude for your sincere and devoted efforts

on behalf of our Association by tendering to you this
emblem of your new office.

◆

I take pleasure in presenting to you on behalf of
your former associates this desk-set as a token of our
respect and admiration for you. May I read the inscription on the marble base? "To our Esteemed Colleague,
John Doe, who, in the years of our association, has won
our sincere respect, our deep affection, and to whom we
extend our warmest wishes for a long life of health and
happiness."

◆

On behalf of the Committee of Awards, it is my
privilege to confer upon you this medal for conspicuous
service in the cause of our servicemen.

◆

The token which I am about to present to you takes
the form of a chest of silver. Will you accept this chest
as a symbol of our gratitude for the hospitality which
you have extended to us on this visit?

◆

We have arranged this meeting for the twofold purpose of saying good-bye to you and offering you some
tangible evidence of our appreciation and goodwill. On
behalf of your fellow officers, I ask you to accept this
token of our esteem.

Illustration 1 — Award

We are proud of this opportunity to honor you for
your achievements. We are here tonight to pay high

tribute to you not only for what you have done but for all that, God willing, you will achieve in the future. There is no doubt that a man of your abilities is destined for even greater accomplishments and higher service. As a token of our very high regard for you we have prepared this illuminated and engraved award for distinguished service. We present it to you with our sincerest good wishes and hope that you will continue your outstanding public service for many more years and in the even broader fields for which you are so ably fitted.

Illustration 2 — Charter

You and your associates have taken on an important and necessary task. You are to be commended on the nobility of your purpose in forming this local union. You are rendering a service to the members of your industry in attempting to improve their working conditions. I congratulate you for your enterprise and unselfishness. It gives me a sense of satisfaction to turn over to you the charter permitting you to function as a labor union. The charter has been duly signed by the appropriate international officers. Many problems beset a new group which will tax your officers and members. I am confident, however, that by applying your combined talents, energies and ingenuity you will solve these problems. I am sure that all of us who are interested in maintaining high standards in the industry will give you and the members of your local union whatever cooperation lies within our power in the furtherance of your commendable purposes.

Illustration 3 — Citation

What makes a good leader? Courage and loyalty, understanding, initiative and vision, and a saving sense of humor. On your 10th anniversary as Secretary of the organization I salute you as an outstanding exponent of all these qualities. It has been, indeed, a privilege to be associated with you and one which I deeply appreciate. As one of the many in whom you evoke the keenest admiration and respect, I take this occasion, on behalf of your brother officers, to present to you this Distinguished Service Award which reads: "To John Doe: Under your inspired leadership our organization has been built up to a high point of efficiency and to a high standard. You have served in many responsible and honored positions. You have given to our organization the benefit of your many attributes with untiring devotion and fidelity. You have lived a life so full of accomplishments that few can match the honor and respect that is associated with your name." It is an honor for me to be chosen to present to you this Distinguished Service Award.

Illustration 4 — Dictionary

Our guest loves words. He uses them well. He can spend whole days with dictionaries. Accordingly, the officers have gotten together to indulge this foible of his and have bought him the best, biggest, and most unabridged dictionary ever printed. I have at the request of the donors inscribed it: "To John Doe: Not that he needs it, but because he knows how to use it better than anyone we know, this book is presented with the affectionate regard and high esteem of all his colleagues."

Illustration 5 — Gavel

You have worked long and diligently in this Lodge and have richly deserved the honor. If I were to attempt to describe adequately the sterling qualities you possess I would infringe upon the time and patience of the other speakers. It gives me pleasure to present to you the gavel which is the emblem of your authority to preside over this lodge. I know you will wield it in a manner which will bring credit to you and honor to the membership. Each time you rap this gavel I know it will be not to demonstrate your authority but to signify the adoption of another progressive step in the fine work of this organization. I have the highest confidence in your ability and I know the success of your administration is assured. It is with pleasure that I tender to you the gavel of authority and the symbol of your new office.

Illustration 6 — Gift

On the 25th anniversary of your service to our organization I express to you appreciation for your loyalty. You have been part of this organization for more than one half of its existence. Through your long years of service you have done your work with the utmost efficiency and dependability. Please accept this little gift as a token of our sincere gratitude for your faithful service. With it go our best wishes for your continued success and happiness for many years to come.

Illustration 7 — Medal

We recognize fully the great service you are rendering to the community. In recognition of these services, I have a very pleasant duty to perform. It is my privilege and delight to make a presentation to you as a mark of appreciation for your unstinting sacrifice of time and effort. It is not often we bestow this medal upon a resident of this community. In this case we feel that no one deserves it more than you. Therefore, on behalf of the community, it is my privilege to present to you the Gold Citizenship Medal. There is an appropriate inscription engraved on it. It reads: "For truly outstanding work to our Community." I ask you to accept this medal from hearts full of gratitude for all you have done.

Illustration 8 — Portrait

In hanging the picture of a true gentleman whose career has been so full of inspiration, whose accomplishments are an outstanding credit to his calling and whose future still lies ahead of him, we perform an act that is and will become even more significant in time to come. What finer tribute can be paid any man than to say he is a gentleman? The word in itself speaks volumes and embodies all those rich traits of character that thrill one with happiness when they are mentioned and more especially when spoken on an occasion such as this. This is a rare and unusual happening since it marks a gracious expression of appreciation which, according to custom, is usually indulged in only after the completion of a man's activities. It is my cherished privilege to present to you this symbol of our affection and love.

Illustration 9 — Scroll

Seldom do we run across a man of better temperament or a more gentlemanly, more considerate and patient one than our secretary. I don't believe that any one of us has ever seen him angry or upset although the Lord knows he must have had plenty of provocation at times. His services for the past 25 years make us so deeply indebted to him that we ought to give him, now that he is retiring, some written evidence of our debt and gratitude to him—some evidence of our appreciation for his long, meritorious and patient work—some token by which to remember us. I, therefore, present this beautifully illuminated scroll, which I now read:

"To John Doe: In acknowledgment and appreciation of the true, faithful and outstanding service rendered by him to our organization in its steady, sound and rapid growth and progress to its present position of influence and prestige. During his secretaryship, no night has been too cold, nor any day too hot, nor any task too difficult for him, whenever an occasion existed to enhance the interests of a member or the organization. His zeal, his personal sacrifices, his devotion and his allegiance to our organization have known no limits. He is respected, honored and beloved by every member and officer of our order. It is our sincere hope and prayer that he may be blessed with health, strength and increased opportunities for even greater achievement in the noble work of our organization." We are certainly going to miss you. Good luck and many years of good health and happiness.

2. Appreciation, Acceptance and Thanks

In your social, community or lodge life you may be the recipient of honors or gifts. You will want to know how to make a brief and interesting speech of acceptance. Say thank you, praise the donor and say something good about the gift or honor. Follow with an expression of acceptance, telling what benefit or pleasure you expect to derive from it.

1. *Expression of Appreciation and Thanks*

It is the greatest honor that has ever been bestowed upon me.

✦

I shall never forget this warm and touching expression of your friendship.

✦

It has aways seemed to me that the greatest honor which can come to a man is to be selected by his brothers for the presidency of their lodge.

✦

I regard the gift of this beautiful gavel as symbolic of the power and might of this organization.

✦

This honor realizes one of my life's ambitions.

✦

I am deeply touched that I am the one upon whom you chose to confer this high honor and all I am able to say at the moment is thank you very much.

✦

I am grateful to you for bringing this beautiful memento all the way across the ocean to present to me.

✦

I have the pleasant duty, in the absence of the Mayor, of participating in these ceremonies and of accepting this magnificent gift on behalf of the citizens of this community.

✦

How can I express the full measure of my appreciation that you have chosen to name this school after me?

I am deeply and sincerely grateful for your considera-tin, courtesy and thought in presenting this traveling bag to me. It is a very appropriate "going-away" gift.

◆

I wish publicly to thank the members for the great honor of electing me to this high office.

◆

I extend my thanks to the organization, the members, and to all who spoke in my behalf, to the president for his confidence in me, and to all of you for coming here.

◆

I thank each of you most heartily for making me so inexpressibly happy by your presence on this impressive and, for me, anyway, memorable occasion.

◆

From the bottom of my heart, I thank my good friends for the kind, congratulatory messages which they have sent to me and the high tributes they have paid me.

◆

I thank the newly elected officers for the kindness, consideration and helpfulness which they have shown me since my elevation and I hope that I may continue to receive the benefit of their experience and wisdom.

◆

With gratitude I acknowledge your message of good wishes and thank you for the many tributes you have paid me. Your friendly sentiments are also heartily appreciated.

◆

It is very pleasant to receive such compliments, espe-cially in the presence of one's wife and parents. But they are so prejudiced in my favor that they are likely to believe all they have heard.

✦

I am grateful, indeed, for the high measure of understanding and support which has been given me.

✦

We thank you with all our hearts for the kind welcome, for the great courtesy, for the generous hospitality, which you have shown us.

2. Acceptance

I accept this appointment with pride but also with a sense of humility. I realize full well the responsibilities and importance of this position, and cherish the opportunity to serve.

✦

I deeply sense the great obligations of this position to which I have been appointed and I shall regard it a duty and privilege to advance your policies with the greatest vigor I possess. With the help of God and the cooperation of the members of this mighty organization I shall devote myself unswervingly toward the attainment of your objectives.

✦

I am fully aware of the magnitude of this office and will do my utmost to discharge my duties with credit to those who have confidence in me and to myself.

✦

It is with a feeling of solemnity and a sense of responsibility that I accept this high honor which you have conferred upon me.

◆

I enter upon my duties with a sense of humility, with appreciation of the attendant responsibilities of the office, and with anxiety lest my abilities fail to keep pace with my eagerness to render the service you expect and to which you are entitled.

◆

It is because this welcome gift from you implies that I am considered worthy, that I will treasure and hold it in the greatest esteem.

Illustration 1 — Award

This realizes one of my life's ambitions. I am proud to be the recipient of this Medal of Distinguished Achievement and I accept it with gratitude and a deep sense of humility. I realize, however, that team spirit, hard work and the loyalty and personal sacrifices of my associates have made this recognition possible. I consider this honor as one in a representative capacity to be shared with all my associates.

Illustration 2 — Gift

Please convey my sincere thanks to the Commander-in-Chief of the VFW for this beautiful token. I interpret this emblem as a present to the officers and members of my organization. It shall be considered by me as a symbol of honor presented by your great organization to the membership of my organization. I want to thank you personally for your fine presentation and your organization for the honor of its visit to us. Please assure your Commander-in-Chief of our continued cooperation and support. We will stand with you in the fight for favorable legislation for veterans and we will work together in the future as we have in the past.

Illustration 3 — Plaque

Thank you for this magnificent plaque. It touches me deeply to be so honored. I shall include this beautiful plaque in my valuable possessions as a common heritage handed to me by representatives of this great fraternal organization. I have really done nothing more than in my own humble way to serve this fine fraternity as best I could. I shall continue to serve as long as I am able.

Illustration 4 — Watch

It would be quite unnatural if I were not deeply touched by this evidence of your good will. I know I will make frequent use of this valuable watch. When I look at it, I will be reminded of the many happy hours I spent in this room. I will recall the time 20 years ago when I was privileged to join the club. This club was then small. Its treasury was insignificant. But its members were enthusiastic and friendly. I will recall the many events that brought the club to the position of influence and prestige that it now enjoys. I will recall the many lasting friendships that began in this club room. I will recall the many happy experiences I enjoyed here. For your thoughtfulness, your kindness, for the sentimental as well as the practical value of your gift, my sincere thanks.

3. Appeal for Funds

In your community or public activities the occasion will frequently arise requiring you to make an appeal, either for funds or for some action. There are two steps in organizing a letter or speech appealing for funds: (1) a statement of the cause, purpose or urgency, and (2) the request for a contribution to the cause or participation in the particular activity, as, for example, voting for the proposition being advocated.

1. Cause, Purpose or Urgency

Cancer has become a national problem which requires national attention and action. No sex or age is safe.

◆

The Cardiac Home is the only place people suffering from heart disease, in desperate need of convalescent care and rehabilitation, can turn to for help.

◆

We respectfully call your attention to the seriousness of the problem of chronic diseases. We wish to emphasize the importance of the work of one of the most needed institutions of its kind in the country—Hope Hospital.

◆

The community strives to provide essential services for the young and the old. Such services include better care for children, summer camps, supervised recreation for youngsters, and programs for the care of the aging.

◆

Not many persons realize the sacrifices your volunteer firemen make to provide fire protection for you. This protection helps to keep your insurance rates down and your taxes lower.

◆

The Police Boys Clubs are important not only to the boys—they are also important to you. They help to keep our community a good place in which to live. The police force knows that a wholesome, friendly respect for law and order must be taught youngsters while they are growing up. Boys who get a chance to know their neighborhood policemen as human beings do not generally turn to juvenile delinquency.

✦

In the Police Athletic League the community has a powerful weapon in the fight against juvenile delinquency. Working at the grass roots level among children who do not belong to any other youth organization, PAL is in a position to prevent delinquency before it gets started.

✦

The high incidence of polio in the past few years has created a national as well as local public health problem. The victims of polio must be aided and the research scientists enabled to continue their work until an effective preventative and cure is found.

✦

If catastrophe strikes, the task of the Red Cross will be gigantic. It must be ready with trained volunteers, nurses, doctors and equipment.

✦

The primary function of the Salvation Army is to fill the gap in services not provided by other organizations. The Army establishes good liaison with churches, schools, fire department associations and clubs so that these organizations may refer to the Army problems which they themselves are not equipped to handle.

✦

It has always been a part of our great American heritage to extend a helping hand to those less fortunate than ourselves. Repeatedly we have taken to our hearts and opened our purses to the sufferers from other lands seeking haven in this country. Is it too much to ask that they be given an opportunity for rehabilitation and a new start in life?

2. *Request for contribution or participation*

This is a cause that merits our generous support, our most devoted efforts. I, therefore, earnestly urge you to send a generous contribution to the campaign. Please send it in today.

✦

It is by your generous contribution that they may be assured of that opportunity. Think of them now and act.

✦

Please add a lonely child—a troubled person—to your Christmas list by sending a special gift to the Fund. It will spread happiness throughout the year.

✦

Will you help us to ameliorate this suffering? Will you make a contribution now to help these children? Enclosed is a leaflet which tells you what we do for needy children and what you can do to help.

✦

Please subscribe as much as you possibly can. Of course, you will be saving yourself a substantial amount of tax money in the end. But your greatest satisfaction will come in knowing that you are giving these children a real, helpful break. Your cooperation will be long remembered.

Your assistance will make larger facilities possible to help those who have not had a chance to develop their bodies. Your contribution helps to sustain not only these children but also ensures that the Community Service will continue to be able to meet the growing needs for its many institutional services in the area.

Our representative in Washington would act to appropriate sufficient funds for the cancer problem if enough Americans showed their concern by writing or wiring to their Congressman. Won't you please write or wire him at once?

I know how many times a year you are called upon for help. I can readily appreciate the strain on your budget. Nevertheless, I ask that you consider giving us a small donation and I assure you personally that these funds will be utilized properly and administered economically.

PAL is now conducting its annual drive to support its many varied activities. This campaign offers the public the opportunity to contribute to a cause which has helped to curb juvenile delinquency and has aided youngsters in building character and good citizenship.

Let us not be too late with too little. We have it within our power to control the destiny of those who have suffered so much. I, therefore, urge you to send a generous contribution to the campaign.

I ask you to show your gratitude to God for your sight by voting for this bill.

Illustration 1 — Blind

Do you realize that 87 percent of our perceptions come through our eyes? This fact tells how much a blind person lost. It tells how important it is for him to have the benefit of help from the rest of us. By careful training the blind can make better use of the perceptions of hearing and touch and thus overcome much of their handicap. Your gift, any amount, will be much appreciated.

Illustration 2 — Blood Donation

A member of my lodge called me. He was frantic and it was with difficulty I got him to talk calmly. His wife was in the hospital bleeding internally from unknown causes. Her bleeding weakened her and she couldn't survive much more loss of blood. She needed a quart of blood each day until her bleeding could be stopped. Would I help? I said, "Of course." Then I reminded myself. My lodge was promoting something known as a blood bank. Some members had contributed blood—enough for a start. Everyone was welcome to use the blood in time of need but he had to pledge to restore a similar quantity. In other words, anybody can borrow blood and have someone repay it later. We have a blank check to draw on the blood bank. The member's wife received all she needed. I am happy to say she is now home and in good condition. If we hadn't had the blood bank the story might not have ended as well as it did. We want more blood in the bank in case we need it. Here's what you do! You, your wife, or any member of your family can go to any Red Cross Blood Donor Station. Tell them, "I want to give blood and I want my lodge to be credited with it." Your biggest sacrifice will be that you must not eat for four hours before you do this. Don't delay too long. You can't tell how badly blood may be needed.

Illustration 3 — Cancer

The enclosed dollar bill, crisp and fresh, should not startle you. We are not giving it away. It is enclosed to dramatize the appeal we are making for the cancer fund. Cancer, as you know, is a terrible scourge upon humanity. It is taking its toll at an alarming rate. The cancer patient needs care, attention, comfort, medication, hospitalization and financial assistance. All too frequently some or all of these needs are denied to him or her by overcrowded hospitals and nursing homes. The cancer fund helps provide all this quickly and efficiently. We are now engaged in a campaign to raise these urgently needed funds. The enclosed dollar bill is to impress you with its importance. Won't you please return it in the enclosed envelope together with your own contribution? Remember, it is better to give a little than nothing at all.

Illustration 4 – Church

Once in a great while a cause so tragic in intensity and so overwhelming in importance is brought to our attention that it transcends any consideration of creed or race. The repair of the damage to our Church as a result of the fire, is such a cause. For 50 years the Church has been a beacon of hope and learning serving the spiritual and communal needs of all residents of the community. We need $50,000 to rebuild the Church. We must insure its continuation for the future. The critical nature of the emergency makes it all the more essential for us to give all we can and as soon as we can. I know that you will not refuse so urgent an appeal. Please mail a generous check with the enclosed blank.

Illustration 5 – Volunteer Fire Department

Your volunteer fire department requires assistance in meeting its operating expenses. Such expenses include death benefits to the beneficiaries of deceased members and cost of recreational and athletic activities, all of which help maintain the morale of the members of your volunteer fire department. Will you please make a generous contribution to those who stand ever ready to make sacrifices for you?

Illustration 6 – Hospital

Almost daily we have been forced to turn away many of the sick and afflicted for lack of the necessary beds and facilities. Hope Hospital must add a new wing to keep pace with the growing demands made upon it for help. Unfortunately, we do not have large endowments but must depend on those who know of the work we have been doing at the hospital for over 50 years. A building fund has been started and we earnestly ask you to add your contribution. We ask of you, in the name of the needy, to give and give more than you have ever given, in gratitude to God for granting you the glorious gift of grace to give, to give to your fellowman, to give for your own self's sake.

Illustration 7 — Needy

You cannot buy happiness. You cannot go to the nearest grocery store and order a pound of happiness as you would a pound of butter. But, since happiness comes from within, you can secure a measure of happiness by your own acts. You can find that feeling of contentment by helping your less fortunate fellowmen. You can help those, who, because of ill-fate, will not have a happy Christmas unless we share with them. During this season of peace and good will, let us not force those in need to look at happiness through our eyes. Rather, let us help them to see and find happiness through their own eyes. Let us not fail the needy and less fortunate of the community.

Illustration 8 — Red Cross

The Red Cross belongs to the people. Major disasters cannot be predicted and when they occur the Red Cross must be ready to throw ample resources into the rescue work. Some of what the Red Cross does is dramatic. A hurricane, a big flood, a burning forest or a burning city stands out as help is mobilized and hurried to the scene. But the Red Cross helps in other ways. If a single burned-out family is in trouble the Red Cross is its neighbor. Disaster service is only one part of the picture. In aiding the veteran and his family, in supplying nursing service, in accident-prevention campaigns, in the national blood donation program, in many other ways, the Red Cross stands ready to minister to all the people. It needs the support of all who can give, and all those who can give only a little can still have the sense of full participation in a great neighborly undertaking.

4. Awards, Citations, Inscriptions, Resolutions, and Scrolls

Awards, citations, inscriptions and scrolls are usually but not necessarily begun by the words:

> "In recognition of"
> "In appreciation of"
> "In tribute to"

then followed by the name of the recipient, words of praise and a brief record of his accomplishments.

Resolutions may be either in simple form beginning "Resolved that" or in the more formal style beginning with the "Whereas" clauses and ending with the "Now, therefore, be it resolved" clause.

A generous amount of material to aid in composing the award, citation, inscription, resolution or scroll is given. Use the material which most nearly applies to your situation and adapt it to your special needs.

Awards, Citations, Inscriptions, Resolutions and Scrolls

(Material for use in awards, citations, inscriptions, resolutions and scrolls.)

✦

He has exercised sound judgment and a wise and kindly counsel and has endeared himself to his associate directors and the office staff.

✦

He is very close to the hearts of his associates who look with pride and satisfaction upon his elevation to the great and exalted position of Grand Master.

✦

He richly deserves the esteem and admiration of his associates. He stands as a shining example of our American way of life. He has conquered handicaps of poverty. Knowing what it means to be poor and underprivileged, he has devoted himself to helping the less fortunate members of our community. We are happy to honor him and we look forward to working with him for the common good and for the welfare of our community for many years to come.

✦

He has rendered efficient, faithful and unobtrusive but invaluable service to our Association.

✦

His passing will leave an unfillable void in the minds and hearts of all those who knew him personally.

✦

For his tireless efforts, unfading loyalty and devotion

on behalf of the fraternity, and the sincere affection he has shown his brothers, we take this occasion on the 25th anniversary of the founding of the fraternity, to tender this scroll as evidence of the high esteem in which he is held by all the members.

✦

For the past 25 years John Doe has rendered faithful, conscientious and valuable services to our organization. Despite the fact that during this period of time, occasions have arisen when his health was impaired, nevertheless, with great personal inconvenience and sacrifice, he carried on his responsibilities. The Board of Directors make formal acknowledgment of its appreciation of the services rendered by him during the years of his leadership and duly acknowledge the substantial contribution which he has made to the organization during the past 25 years. It is the sincere hope of the members, officers and Board of Directors that he will enjoy many more years of good health and happiness.

✦

John Doe, as president of this organization, served for many years with loyalty, honor and distinction; in his official acts he was governed by a keen sense of duty and always showed a unique grasp of human problems; he always sought to aid his fellowman in an hour of need, and for these reasons he gained and maintained the admiration, esteem and affection of members and his colleagues. Therefore, we herewith give expression on behalf of the members of our sense of loss and deep regret on his retirement and extend our best wishes to him for a long and happy life.

For his leadership in gaining public support for the national program of education and service so vitally needed to combat a serious threat to the nation's health. . . . . .

◆

We do appreciate the energy, the enthusiasm, the resourcefulness and the skill with which you served as campaign chairman for the March of Dimes drive. We hereby salute you for the success that crowned your efforts in this noble community project.

◆

His humanitarian sympathies and inspiring efforts during the national campaign to gain public support for research, education and community service made him the individual most responsible for the successful initiation of the program so essential to our nation's health. In recognition of all this, the testimonial is awarded with grateful appreciation.

◆

The Board of Directors extend to you, John Doe, on your birthday, July fifth, many good wishes for your health, happiness and prosperity. It is our fervent hope that you be spared for many years to come so that you may continue to guide the Board of Directors.

◆

In appreciation of the rich contribution made by the Tribunal to the common objectives of enlightened thinking and democratic living through the medium of intelligent, fair-minded journalism.

◆

Sincerely, quietly, modestly and with grace and dignity has John Doe demonstrated his patriotism and his deep interest in the welfare of the members. For his generosity and loyalty to them; for his graciousness, devotion, courtesy and help to the members of the Association, and his many acts of public service, this testimonial is given by his brethren.

◆

His passionate interest in life was to see that the individual was given the freedom to be heard; and to this end he fought relentlessly against all forms of censorship, intolerance, and political, social and economic oppression. He had the courage of his convictions and the ability to exercise them.

◆

Eminent statesman, distinguished teacher, editor and author in the fields of history and political science. Man of noble spirit, humanitarian principles, and one who possesses a compassionate understanding of the suffering and persecuted. His high moral integrity, lofty ideals, broad sympathies, and unselfish devotion to democratic principles has won for him the love and affection of freedom-loving people throughout the world. Saintly in character, liberal in spirit and vigorous in mind.

◆

The Association, cognizant of the unique part Mary Doe has played in advancing its power and prestige, delights to record in this her 6oth year the affection and grateful regard in which she is held by all of its officers and members, and to express to her their best wishes for continued health and happiness.

Illustration 1 — Resolution of Praise

RESOLVED, that the Executive Board recognize the long services rendered by John Doe in the various positions held by him in this organization, and appreciating his faithful services therein for the past fifteen years, wishes him all the happiness he so justly merits by his good and loyal conduct during his long connection with it.

RESOLVED, that this resolution be entered into the minutes and a copy be presented to John Doe.

Illustration 2 — Resolution of Praise

WHEREAS, this month marks the completion of the 5th year Reverend John Doe has served Hope Church as its spiritual leader, and

WHEREAS, during these five years Hope Church has expanded its physical facilities with the addition of a new community center and schoolhouse, and has enlarged its services to members and their families, and has extended the curriculum of the religious school, and

WHEREAS, this growth on the part of Hope Church has been due in large measure to the inspiration, zeal, devotion and leadership of Reverend John Doe,

NOW, THEREFORE, BE IT RESOLVED that we, the Board of Trustees of Hope Church, do hereby express our sincere thanks and appreciation to Reverend John Doe for his achievements on behalf of our Church, and it is further

RESOLVED, that this resolution be spread on the minutes of this meeting, be published in the next issue of the Bulletin and also be read at the next annual meeting of the congregation.

Illustration 3 — Resolution of Praise

WHEREAS, John Doe has completed 25 years of service as President of Local 234, and

WHEREAS, by his zeal and generous labors he has helped to improve the working conditions of our members, and by his dignity and sterling character gained the love and esteem of his devoted brothers,

NOW, THEREFORE, BE IT RESOLVED, that the entire membership unite in giving this testimonial to their beloved and honored president as a token of heart·felt appreciation for his untiring efforts.

Illustration 4 — Resolution to Aid Charity

WHEREAS, The Medical Center has always supported the March of Dimes to help fight infantile paralysis, and

WHEREAS, a great majority of those afflicted must look to the National Foundation of Infantile Paralysis throughout the country to provide funds for medical and hospital care to help them on the road to recovery, and

WHEREAS, this care is being provided regardless of age, race, creed or color,

BE IT RESOLVED, by The Medical Center, that we commend to our members the March of Dimes drive for special and extraordinary support, individually and collectively.

Illustration 5 — Resolution of Thanks to Press

WHEREAS, the press has lived up to its highest tradition of accuracy, fairness and comprehensiveness in its coverage of this conference,

THEREFORE, BE IT RESOLVED, that this organization go on record as expressing its deepest thanks to the press.

Illustration 6 — Resolution of Thanks for Hospitality

Resolved, that most cordial thanks be tendered to the Association for the kindly welcome and generous hospitality which have been extended to the delegates, and for the arrangements which have been made for their further reception and entertainment at the places to be visited in the coming weeks. It would be impossible adequately to express the gratitude felt by every member of the delegation for the kindness which has been showered upon all. The delegates can only ask the Association to believe that the sentiments now recorded are expressed with the deepest sincerity and in the hope that they will be regarded as strengthening, renewing and extending the many friendships which were made here.

Illustration 7 — Resolution of Thanks

WHEREAS, John Doe has rendered loyal and faithful services as president for the past ten years, and before that as a loyal member, and

WHEREAS, he has exhibited marked ability, deep interest and uniform attentiveness and has fulfilled his office with credit, and

WHEREAS, the Executive Board wishes to express the sincere appreciation it and the membership feels for the fine and faithful services rendered by John Doe,

THEREFORE, BE IT RESOLVED, that John Doe is deserving of the tributes paid to him, and further,

RESOLVED, that a copy of this resolution be printed in the Souvenir Journal to be published in connection with the Testimonial Dinner to be tendered to John Doe.

Illustration 8 — Resolution of Tribute

WHEREAS, it has been the Will of Almighty God to remove from amongst us Brother John Doe who has been a most valued member, ever active in the affairs of the Club since 1928; one who throughout the years has served the Club loyally, generously and unselfishly,

THEREFORE, BE IT RESOLVED, that the Officers and Board of Governors do hereby record this expression of sincere and enduring grief which has been sustained by the Club of which he was so faithful and prominent a member.

5. Testimonials

Frequently a testimonial dinner is tendered to a deserving person. In conjunction with the dinner a souvenir journal is often printed. Testimonials or greetings, which are messages of praise and tribute, are printed in the journal. Examples of such testimonials are given below.

Illustration 1

It is a privilege to extend to John Doe our sincere greetings in recognition of his many years of faithful service to the organization which he heads. He has served his membership faithfully and deserves the high esteem in which he is held. On behalf of my organization, I extend sincere greetings to him and all those in attendance at this Testimonial Dinner.

Illustration 2

I have known John Doe for the past ten years and have worked with him during that time. His diligent and courageous efforts to bring about better conditions in the industry have been eminently successful. It is because of men like John Doe that we have prospered and I cannot let pass this opportunity to express my sincere appreciation of his achievements. This is my testimonial to a good, sincere labor official.

Illustration 3

I consider it a privilege to greet you on the occasion of this splendid dinner in your honor. During the years I have had contact with you, I have learned to respect the ability and good sense you have brought to your work. As a leader of your community, you have demonstrated courage and vision. Whether at the conference table, in private meetings, or on the platform, your measured words have always produced a keen respect for your wishes and warm, human understanding. I am happy to join with your many good friends in paying tribute to you this evening.

Illustration 4

We send you our warmest congratulations on the occasion of your 25th anniversary and the testimonial tendered to you in celebration of that event. You can well be proud of your quarter century of service. Accept our best wishes for your continued success.

Illustration 5

Congratulations and many happy returns of the day are my wishes for your 25th anniversary. It is not the years a man has lived, but how much he has accomplished, that indicates his usefulness. You are blessed with an irrepressible spirit and a dynamic energy, transmitting your power to others. This is proved by the enviable reputation, influence and prestige of the organization of which you have been such an important part. May you continue to enjoy splendid health.

Illustration 6

It is to you, John Doe, our first president, that we owe the existence of our Association. You were the founder. It was in your brain that the idea of founding an association germinated. To carry out that purpose, you gathered around you a group of distinguished persons whose labors culminated in the organization of the Association. Your interest in the group has never wavered. You have been the guiding hand throughout those vital, formative years. This testimonial is a fitting ribute to you.

Illustration 7

The excellent work done by Mr. John Doe during the many years of his leadership of your organization clearly warrants this Testimonial Dinner. The strength and recognition attained by the organization are a silent tribute to his able efforts.

6. Announcements of Meetings and Functions

In group activities the occasion to tender a testimonial dinner to a deserving person is a frequent occurrence.

The requirements of a letter or statement announcing a testimonial dinner, a meeting or other function are a statement of (1) the purpose, cause or occasion, and (2) the invitation or request to participate.

Illustrations of letters and statements normally used for such occasions appear in this chapter. The complete illustrations follow the material in Step one and Step two.

1. The purpose, cause or occasion

To provide funds for the maintenance and upkeep of the club and to insure a continuance of entertaining monthly meetings, a souvenir journal will be printed in conjunction with our Annual Installation and Dinner.

◆

Here's a chance to have a good time enjoying one of the season's funniest comedies and at the same time help the Community Fund. As you have doubtless guessed, it is a theatre party. The show is "Community Antics," written by Richard Jones.

◆

Once again the opportunity is afforded us as members of the community to participate in its charitable activities. Just such an activity is the dinner which is being given in honor of Sam Brown, on behalf of our hospital fund.

◆

On May 19th at 5:00 P.M. we will have a meeting at the Hotel Main and we want you with us. The purpose of this meeting is to discuss a plan we have formulated to "do something" for our president. We know you are among those who respect and admire our president. We need help to carry out this plan.

2. The invitation or request to participate

It is a real pleasure to extend to you a most cordial invitation to attend your school's Charter Day Celebration to be held in the Main Hall on November 12th at 6:00 P.M.

◆

Since I know that you are a personal friend of our guest of honor, it is my pleasure to extend to you and your wife a cordial invitation to be our guests and enjoy the evening with us at that time.

◆

Please do your utmost to attend and bring with you any of your friends who would be willing to assist us. We want this afternoon to be the beginning of the most successful campaign our community has had. Your presence will help assure this.

◆

The contribution you make above the box office price helps the sick and needy.

◆

I urge you, therefore, in order to help us pay proper tribute to him, to let me know on the enclosed card that you will be with us at his testimonial dinner on December 1st.

◆

I would like, therefore, to have you join us on December 1st, at the Plaza. There will be no engraved invitations and no fund raising. Tickets are $5. We have less than a month to do it in. You know how we put off send-in reservations and such. Would you be good enough to return yours today. Thanks a lot and please let me hear from you.

You may obtain tickets by sending your check to the theatre. Those who cannot find it convenient to attend, may be inspired to make a donation to the Foundation.

◆

Your participation in the past has proved that you are willing to extend your help to the needy. Your active help is needed to make the campaign successful.

The need this year is greater than ever before and we feel that we can rely upon your coöperation to help us make this year's drive an outstanding success.

This is a purely voluntary proposition. Nobody is going to be asked to work or contribute funds unless he offers to do so.

◆

The committee urges every member to attend the December 1st meeting. At this meeting a vote will be taken to determine whether the club favors the establishment of a Housing Authority. If you find it impossible to attend, please cast your vote by returning the enclosed card.

Illustration 1 — Testimonial

I know you will be pleased to learn that a testimonial dinner will be tendered to our esteemed president, Mr. John Doe, on the completion of ten years of service to the Sutton Association. The dinner will be held at the Plaza Hotel on December 1st. Mr. Doe has demonstrated time and again a deep understanding of our problems, and by a fair and just administration he has won the respect and affection of everyone. When the idea for a testimonial dinner was first advanced, the response was so spontaneous and so overwhelming that the plan soon became an accomplished fact. I know that you and your wife will want to join us in doing honor to Mr. Doe.

The dinner will be a delicious one with music, dancing, and a minimum of speeches. Tickets are $10 per person, with the net proceeds going to a charitable organization. Let me know the number of tickets you desire by filling in and returning the enclosed card. Tickets are selling rapidly and the committee wants to make proper allocation of the limited number of reservations available. Let me hear from you very soon, please.

Illustration 2 — Reserve Now!

Because of the splendid coöperation of the members, the outlook for the John Doe testimonial dinner is most favorable. In fact, the possibility is strong that we will be oversubscribed. It would be very unfortunate if we had to turn down any member who wishes to be with us on that gala night. We cannot overcrowd the room. 350 will be our limit. That number can be handled comfortably. Please mark this: We have reservations for over 250. If it is your intention to attend, please send in your reservation early. Mail it to Secretary Smith.

Illustration 3 — Ad for Journal

On Saturday evening, December 1st, the Sutton Association is sponsoring its 20th Annual Entertainment and Dance at the Plaza Hotel. This year we are honoring John Doe's ten years of devoted and loyal service to the association. In connection with the dance we are printing a souvenir journal. A contract for the journal is enclosed. We feel confident that you will want to be represented in this journal. Please return the contract with your remittance to the journal chairman, Mr. Walter Whalen.

Illustration 4 — Greeting for Journal

The Craft Union is tendering a testimonial dinner to Robert Roe, its president, on the occasion of his completion of ten years of service to it. A souvenir journal is being published in connection with the event. You have met Mr. Roe on many occasions, and have had frequent contact with him, particularly during the last mayoralty campaign. It would be appropriate to print your message of greeting to him as Mayor of this city in the souvenir journal. We would appreciate it if you would forward your copy to us so that we can send it to the printer no later than December 1st.

Illustration 5 — Appreciation for Good Wishes

On behalf of the Sutton Association I wish to thank you for your message of congratulations and good wishes upon the occasion of your 20th Anniversary. Your letter symbolizes the fine spirit of friendship and cooperation between our organizations and it is most sincerely appreciated.

Illustration 6 — From Guest of Honor

I am the guest of honor at the charity dinner to be held in the Community Center on Wednesday evening, December 7, at 7 P.M. Ordinarily, when arrangements are being made for an occasion such as this, the guest of honor should be seen but not heard. But everybody knows that charity dinners are different. Here, I am merely a symbol for something more important. The Fund needs money to enable it to carry out its program to maintain the institution for which it is responsible. I appeal to you to consider the problem of the Fund when making your contribution. A reservation card for the dinner is enclosed. Your check made out to the Fund should be in the amount of $5 for each person attending the dinner. I look forward to greeting you there.

Illustration 7 — Dinner Schedule

Final arrangements have been made to assure the outstanding success of the testimonial dinner to Robert Roe. So that you may derive the fullest enjoyment from the evening's events, your coöperation is solicited. All guests must arrive at the ballroom of the hotel no later than 6:30 P.M. on Saturday, December 1st. Dinner will be served promptly at 7 P.M. This schedule must be maintained so that the events of the evening can go on as planned. Yours for a memorable evening.

Illustration 8 – Reservation Acknowledgment

Thank you for your reservations for the dinner in honor of John Doe on December 1st, 6:30 P.M. in the Plaza Hotel. We appreciate the support that you are giving the community and we are sure that the dinner will be made more impressive by your attendance. Please remind your friends about the dinner as it promises to be a memorable tribute to John Doe and a helping hand to the community. Once again, thanks.

Illustration 9 – Reservation Reminder

We have not yet received your reservation to join us at the Plaza Hotel the evening of December 1st to do honor to John Doe for his services to the community. We believe this must be an oversight on your part. Final reservations must be made at least thirty days in advance. Your committee was given until November 15th to pay for all the reservations. We are enclosing a reservation blank and postpaid envelope for your convenience. We would appreciate it very much if you will fill in your reservation and mail it, together with a check payable to the undersigned. We anticipate the pleasure of seeing you at the dinner.

Illustration 10 — Serve on Reception Committee

I have been asked by the officers and directors of the Sutton Association to serve as chairman of the testimonial dinner to honor John Doe. I am writing to ask you to serve on the reception committee to pay a suitable tribute to our guest of honor who has done so much for so many people. The proceeds of this dinner will be contributed to the Fund to erect a clubhouse for thousands of boys in this and neighboring communities. Please let me have your acceptance. Your coöperation will be a source of encouragement to us.

Illustration 11 — Serve as Sponsor

On the occasion of John Doe's 10th Anniversary of service to the community, the members of the Sutton Association and his friends are tendering to him a testimonial dinner. It would be an honor to have you join with us as a sponsor of this dinner and to have your permission to place your name upon our letterhead. The dinner is to be held on December 1st at the Plaza Hotel and I am sure you will want to join us. Your coöperation will aid immeasurably in insuring the success of this affair. We anxiously await your reply.

7. Speech Openings

The audience's first impression is the speaker's chief concern. As he walks on to the platform, greets his audience, gives his first sentences, the audience is forming their first impression of him. He must win the approval of his audience for himself and his subject. The beginning should establish a friendly relationship between speaker and audience and arouse their interest in his subject and its development.

In the next few pages will be found sufficient speech openings to meet the demands of almost any normal situation and help the speaker off to a good start.

It is certainly gracious of you to listen to me at this very late hour. I, in turn, will be as brief as possible in discussing this tremendously important subject now under consideration.

✦

It is hardly necessary for me to say that I consider it a very great honor to be asked to occupy this platform for a few moments.

✦

I appreciate very much this opportunity to meet with you men and women, and I am deeply grateful for the confidence and for the honor that you have done me.

✦

I am deeply honored by the invitation extended to me to address you this evening. It is always a pleasure to come here. I have pleasant memories of my visit about a year ago when I was a guest at your round table conference. I remember vividly the difficult questions that some of you asked then and I hope that I am prepared to answer a few more tonight.

✦

I fully appreciate that at this hour, and after the entertaining addresses we have listened to, it would be an imposition to attempt to hold your attention except for the briefest time.

✦

I regard the privilege of addressing you as imposing upon me two obligations: first, that of being brief; second, that of saying such things only as are calculated to merit the attention of men whose time is as precious as yours is. For breach of the first obligation I should be without excuse but the second involves such difficulties that I must rely upon your kind forbearance if I fall short.

✦

When I have recovered, Mr. Chairman, from your kind but too generous introduction I will, I hope, get my mind sufficiently cleared to make a few pertinent remarks.

✦

It would be very difficult, indeed, for me to express adequately my appreciation of the honor which has been conferred upon me by inviting me to address this great gathering.

✦

We are about to perform one of the most sacred rites incidental to our membership in this great organization, that is, the installation of our newly elected officers.

✦

These induction proceedings are becoming quite a habit, but I think they are very proper because they express the desire of the organization to pay tribute to one who richly deserves the honor.

✦

Agreeable to the established tradition of this organization, the president is expected to make a report. The hour has now come. With your indulgence, I will do so, and I think within 15 minutes it will be over.

✦

I deeply appreciate the privilege of addressing the organization from which in so short a time and from such humble beginnings this vast, influential and strong association has grown. This organization has prestige; it has strength. May it always continue to use its position for the common good!

♦

It is good to be home again. As I have gone about the state I have had many cordial welcomes and friendly receptions but none has touched me as deeply as the heartwarming greetings from my friends and neighbors in this town. There is no place like home.

♦

It is a great joy for me today to be here to introduce the speakers on this very delightful occasion.

My function is to act as presiding officer and to introduce to this audience those who have asked to participate and give expression on this occasion of their regard and affection for our guest of honor.

♦

I have called this conference at this time for the three-fold purpose of, first, meeting you personally and giving you an opportunity to look over your new president; second, to outline briefly the policy I shall adopt in the administration of the organization; third, to set forth the results of my survey of the organization to date and the initial steps upon which I have decided.

♦

I have attended enough conventions to know how you feel after a week of it. You have visited all the museums, art galleries and other cultural monuments of the city and you are beginning to weary. And, of course, you have to listen to speeches, too. I console myself with the thought that this punishment, while cruel, is not unusual.

We are embarking tonight upon a new venture, the formation of a civic group for the purpose of protecting and advancing the interests of the residents and to foster a healthy interest in the civic affairs of the community. Since we are all bound together by a desire to make our community a friendly and wholesome place in which to live and bring up our children, we are all hopeful that our common goal will be attained.

✦

This is the 10th annual dinner, and with no immodesty, it can be said that we have grown in membership, and have become stronger in prestige and influence.

✦

We have met for a special purpose tonight and that is to honor a man whom we all esteem and love, a man who has had a distinguished career. The sentiments of the Association will later be expressed by the one selected for that purpose.

✦

You may have noticed that on our program we have the song we all love so well, "America," and I am going to ask you, after the first toast, to sing that song. I now ask you to rise and drink to the President of the United States.

✦

All of us are agreed that more participation by the citizens in public affairs is not only desirable but imperative. The problem we are here to discuss is how we can achieve that—by what ways and means.

✦

The distinct privilege of opening this pleasant ceremony has been accorded me and naturally I must be brief because of the speakers who are to follow.

◆

It has indeed been a cherished privilege that was accorded me to be the presiding officer of these ceremonies.

◆

I would like to render a somewhat free-style account of my brief stewardship as the Secretary of the organization.

◆

If you will permit me, I will use these few notes, not to encourage the expansion of my remarks but as an anchor to keep me nailed down to a short space of time.

8. Addresses of Welcome

As the presiding officer or his designee you welcome guests and members. It is your duty to be gracious. In most cases you will be acting as spokesman for a group. Make it clear that the greeting comes from all and not from you alone. There are several examples of addresses of welcome in the next few pages. Almost any one of them can be adapted to your needs.

Illustration 1

I want to assure you that our welcome to you is warm
and heartfelt. We hope you will enjoy our city and that
the friendships made here may grow and deepen. We
hope you will have time to enjoy many of the unrivaled
beauty spots of the state and its many facilities for
recreation. We want to do everything possible to make
your visit here memorable. We hear so often that the
city is a cold place—but those who live here know that
this is not true. We have made arrangements to show
you the warmth of hospitality that exists here. May your
gathering here be a successful and enjoyable one!

Illustration 2

The Community welcomes you to her heart with all
the warmth and fervor which she accords to the home-
coming of her own sons and daughters, among whom
you are numbered by adoption during the next few
days. We hope that your meetings will be so marked
with success that you will immediately begin making
plans for a return visit to this community. It is our hope
that your deliberations may be fruitful of good to all
of the peoples represented and that lasting friendships
may here be cemented. We greet you not as strangers,
not as mere acquaintances, but as friends. We want you
to know that we will do everything in our power to
make your stay here a pleasant one.

Illustration 3

We are indeed very grateful that you are here. We hope you will enjoy yourselves and that you will return to your homes with pleasant recollections of what you have seen and done here. If there is anything that we can do which we have not already done to make your visit more pleasant, we are yours to command. To be a host to such a gathering is an honor of which any community might well be proud.

Illustration 4

It is a very great pleasure for me, as the Mayor, to extend to you the warm welcome of this City. You have many problems to consider. A glance at your agenda is sufficient to indicate the range. You have not only a heavy task but a great responsibility. Many eyes are upon you today. I hope you will find here the satisfaction and guidance that you wish for, and that your meetings will meet with every success.

Illustration 5

I am performing here today one of the pleasantest tasks of my career: that is, welcoming you to this distinguished organization. It is going to be a pleasant association. I am sure that the organization has never responded more warmly to any appointment than it has to yours. I am sure that the staff will serve under your direction with the greatest of pleasure and with full coöperation. To have you as a co-officer is a matter of great personal satisfaction to your new colleagues.

9. Introductions

The object is to create a desire to hear the speaker you are introducing. The situation requires a brief statement of the speaker's background, his qualifications for handling the subject, and his name. Laudatory remarks are appropriate but should not be overdone. In this chapter are examples of complimentary remarks followed by illustrations of introductions.

HOW TO INTRODUCE IMPORTANT PERSONS

Governor (out of his own state)	"The Governor" "The Governor of New Jersey
Mayor	"Mayor Jones"
Senator (U.S. or State)	"Senator Sampson"
Member of Congress (or State Legislature)	"Mr. Brown, Congressman from Georgia"
Cardinal	"His Eminence, Cardinal Stanton"
Roman Catholic Archbishop (There is no Archbishop in U.S.)	"The Most Reverend, The Archbishop of Chicago"
Bishop (either Roman Catholic or Protestant)	"Bishop Land"

Priest	"The Reverend Father Delaney"
Monsignor	"Monsignor Hogan"
Protestant Clergyman	"Mr. Kirk"
(if D.D. or LL.D.)	"Dr. Kirk"
(if Lutheran)	"Pastor Kirk"
Rabbi	"Rabbi Lane"
(if D.D. or LL.D.)	"Dr. Lane"

Examples of Complimentary Remarks

He is a man of science, learning and skill. His profound knowledge and experience have won for him widespread recognition in his profession. Like many men of accomplishment, he is unaffected and unassuming.

◆

He has performed his official duties with unswerving integrity and fearless determination. His forthright, frank and honest attitude in relation to public matters stamps him as being destined for higher office and responsibilities.

◆

He gives lavishly of his time and effort. His sincerity and integrity have earned him the respect and admiration of all of us.

◆

We are aware that many men who attain high positions continually grow in stature. From the very beginning the career of our next speaker has been one of continuous growth.

He has always been a champion of civic betterment and a tireless advocate of honest government.

✦

He represents a rare combination of judgment, social imagination, immunity to pressure, and fidelity to truth.

✦

Under his leadership we can look forward to a brilliant future and increased success for our association.

✦

He is a fluent speaker, a man of extraordinary vitality and great administrative ability. He is certain to be a source of strength to the administration in the solution of its problems.

✦

He has a knack of taking the audience into his confidence and no audience is proof against his expansive charm.

✦

Through her intellectual force and the warmth of her understanding she has done much to explain the international scene to her audience.

✦

We all admire his penetrating insight into the complexities of the international situation. He is indeed a most remarkable journalist.

✦

His contribution to a better understanding of Europe's problems will not be forgotten. He brings to the muddled international affairs a clarity of thinking and interpretation which is unmatched.

He has performed his arduous tasks with a seriousness, a sense of responsibility, and a feeling for the gravity of the issues involved which deserves the highest praise.

✦

His industry and sincerity have made for him a host of friends and have earned the respect of his colleagues.

✦

He is a man of great character and wonderful temperament who enjoys a splendid reputation for integrity, honesty, and loyalty.

✦

He has many attributes of the successful advocate: a fine presence, quick wit, commanding eloquence, and an enormously persuasive manner.

✦

He is a champion of unpopular causes; a man who never lets the prevailing opinion divert him even an inch from the course he thinks is right.

✦

He has demonstrated his warm-hearted humanity and deep concern for the welfare of his fellowman by unceasing service and devotion to myriad philanthropic causes.

Illustration 1

In introducing the Mayor, I present to you a man who at all times has championed the interests of the civil employee. He has never hesitated to make known his sympathy for the white-collar class, nor has his stand ever been a source of embarrassment to his administration. I am pleased to present Mayor Jones.

Illustration 2

It is a great honor to have with us the Governor of the State of New Jersey. In addition to gracing this occasion by his personal presence, it is a special tribute to our guest of honor. Governor Brown, we welcome you here as a true friend. We are honored to have you with us. It is a privilege to call upon you at this moment. Ladies and Gentlemen, the Governor of New Jersey.

Illustration 3

We are to have the pleasure of meeting and listening to an address by Senator Weston. He responded to our invitation with refreshing speed and enthusiasm. He is a great American, a distinguished member of the Senate and a good friend. I present Senator Weston.

Illustration 4

I am happy to present to you a newly elected member of Congress who made a great campaign when the odds were much against him. I present Mr. Wilson, Congressman from Ohio.

Illustration 5

The next speaker is one of the honored gentlemen of this community. He is widely known as one who has held many important offices and who continues to hold public office. He is a member of the State legislature. I take pleasure in presenting Mr. Samuel Shield.

Illustration 6

I have the great privilege of presenting the Most Reverend, The Archbishop of San Francisco. He is a highly regarded representative of a great religious organization. He is a philosopher, a scholar, and a humanitarian. He has built up to a high point of efficiency the splendid diocese over which he presides. He is loved by all people, regardless of religious affiliation. He belongs to all of us. The Most Reverend, The Archbishop of San Francisco.

Illustration 7

We are fortunate in having the Reverend Father Delaney as guest speaker for our meeting. The subject of his talk is one of which he is exceptionally well qualified to speak, with both wisdom and authority. I know we shall have a stimulating evening. The Reverend Father Delaney.

Illustration 8

I present Bishop Land who will pronounce the benediction.

Illustration 9

I am happy to present Rabbi Lane who has spoken to us before. On the other occasion he made a most favorable and lasting impression upon our hearts and minds.

Illustration 10

I present a member of the Board of Chaplains, Pastor Brown, for the opening prayer. Pastor Brown.

Illustration 11

I now give the audience the real gift of the occasion, the man you have been waiting to hear, our guest of honor, John Doe.

Illustration 12

It is particularly appropriate to have with us tonight a devoted colleague of our guest of honor. I know he did not expect to be called upon, but may I invade his privacy to ask him to say a few words, or take a bow. Mr. Fred Frost.

Illustration 13

Our secretary has rendered most valuable services to our organization. No man has served with a greater degree of integrity and sincerity. We cannot appraise adequately the value of his services, but it far exceeds the compensation we pay him. I present Mr. Samuel Wright.

Illustration 14

I would like to pay my respects to Mr. Bernard Banks, our treasurer. I have had the good fortune of knowing

him for many years. I doubt if any organization has a
better watchdog of the exchequer than we have. He is
what a treasurer should be. He is constantly on his guard
to see that no money is spent foolishly. I hope he will
consent to address you. Mr. Banks.

Illustration 15

I present to you the able, industrious, and efficient
chairman of the ways and means committee, for his report. Mr. Robert Roe.

Illustration 16

We consider it a matter of great good fortune that
Professor Stanton has agreed to deliver the first annual
lecture. At the risk of carrying coals to Newcastle, I
will give you a brief recital of the high points in the
career of this distinguished scholar. Professor Stanton is
the recipient of last year's scientific award. He represented American engineering and education organizations
at two international conferences abroad during this year.
He is the president-general of the International Congress
on Coastal Engineering. It is with great pleasure and a
deep consciousness of privilege that I introduce the lec-
turer, Professor Stanton.

Illustration 17

I am sure that our distinguished visitor fully appreci-
ates the warmth of the welcome you have extended to

him. I can assure him that we are tremendously happy because he is here. He is associated with the liberal, progressive, forward-looking people of our country. I am pleased to present Sir William Church.

Illustration 18

Mr. Samuel Sampson has traveled a long way to bring you a message that will be both scholarly and interesting. He comes here especially qualified to speak to us upon the subject. I present Mr. Samuel Sampson.

Illustration 19

I know you have been looking forward with pleasant and happy anticipation to the message of a great American. He came here at a great personal sacrifice. I want to assure him we are pleased and happy to have him with us. I take great pleasure in presenting Mr. John Jones.

Illustration 20

What shall I say about Alfred Alton? That he is a gifted actor? Shall I enumerate the enormous range of parts he has portrayed? The names of the Broadway hits in which he has made theatrical history? Shall I tell you he holds audiences spellbound and that this should be a truly thrilling experience? Any attempt on my part to embellish Mr. Alton's accomplishments with superlatives is unnecessary. His very presence projects his personality. I know what I shall say to you. It is my great privilege to present Mr. Alfred Alton.

Illustration 21

The chair recognizes a most beloved member of the community, who by his own character and attainments, is most worthy to eulogize the late John Doe. I present Richard Roe.

10. Thanking the Speaker

At the conclusion of the speaker's address it is the obligation of the chairman to thank him briefly and graciously. On the following pages are examples of remarks which may be used by the chairman to express appreciation and thanks.

Illustration 1

The audience has indicated in an impressive manner
its appreciation of your eloquent and entertaining
address. And it was thought-provoking, too. We thank
you also for that graciousness, that friendliness of manner
which has given so much charm to every moment of
your presence with us.

Illustration 2

We are deeply indebted to you for your statesman-
like address. Although I have heard many good talks,
I can say sincerely without any attempt at flattery that
we have just listened to one of the most constructive
and thoughtful speeches, on a subject of major interest,
that has been delivered in many years.

Illustration 3

Thank you, Mr. Brown, for your excellent talk and
the sincere way in which you delivered it. I know your
message has made a deep impression upon our con-
sciences.

Illustration 4

I am sure that I voice the unanimous sentiment of this
meeting when I thank Mr. Brown for his contribution
to a verv perplexing problem.

Illustration 5

I know we are all deeply impressed by the address of Mr. Smith. It touches us very deeply. He has left an imprint upon our memories which will remain with us for a long, long time.

Illustration 6

Much light has been shed by Mr. Doe on the confusing questions of foreign policy. We all liked his sincere, outspoken and courageous thinking and his refusal to succumb to mob hysteria. Your sincere attentiveness is eloquent appreciation of his talk. Thanks to him for his brilliant and courageous dissertation and thanks to you for being such an excellent and responsive audience.

Illustration 7

You have indicated your appreciation of the masterful address delivered by Congressman Brown better than I could. The people of this district are to be congratulated upon the exercise of fine judgment in electing this splendid, keen and vigorous man as their representative. He has shown vision and an understanding of our problems. The manner in which he delivered his message was most impressive and convincing. I predict for him a great future. We thank you profoundly for your address.

Illustration 8

I wish to add my words of thanks for the very notable talk delivered by Mr. Smith. The particular value of his address lies in the fact that his opinions result from an intimate knowledge of the facts and his experience with concrete cases.

Illustration 9

Senator, the audience has manifested its feelings of appreciation for your eloquent address by the volume of applause. We are grateful to you for your visit with us. Thank you.

Illustration 10

Thank you for expressing so eloquently the feeling that we have for a great leader.

11. Nominations

The elements of a nomination speech are (1) a statement of the qualifications of the candidate, and (2) the placing in nomination.

The nomination should be simple and concise. Under some circumstances, when the qualifications of the candidate are well known, the plain statement, "I nominate John Doe for President," is sufficient.

Material giving parliamentary procedure, and for composing the more embellished speech of nomination is given in this chapter, followed by complete illustrations.

PARLIAMENTARY PROCEDURE

CHAIRMAN: Nominations are now in order.

MEMBER: I nominate John Doe for president (or states qualifications and places in nomination).

(Nominations need not be seconded.)

CHAIRMAN: Are there any other nominations?

MEMBER: I move that nominations be closed.

CHAIRMAN: There being no objection, nominations are closed and we shall proceed to vote.

(After the vote, the newly elected president takes the chair and says: "Nominations are in order for vice-president." In the same manner the other officers are elected.)

1. Qualifications of candidate

There are certain requirements that the leadership of an organization of a thousand members must have and among these qualifications is that humble touch, that down-to-earth approach to problems. John Doe has these qualifications.

◆

He is a champion of minorities, a defender of human rights. He has often raised his voice against bigotry and intolerance. He is loved and revered by members of this organization. He is an asset to it.

◆

Time does not permit me to give a recital of the abilities and accomplishments of the man I desire to place in nomination but I think you know them as well as I do. Ten years ago you elected him secretary. He has served you ably, honestly and capably.

◆

It is not my purpose to deliver an oration regarding his qualifications because they are all well known. He has always placed his great talents at the service of his organization whenever there was a call to duty.

◆

He has been a distinguished public official but that is only part of the story. In both his public and private life he has demonstrated a deep and abiding feeling for those whose opportunities have been limited by circumstances or by cruel conditions imposed on them by events beyond their control. He has more than outstanding ability; he has a sense of compassion. The two together give him his distinction. They explain his sense of kinship with us and ours with him.

◆

It is significant that he has always served in positions where he could help people. The desire to do so must run very deep in the grain of his personality and beliefs. I do not believe that much more can be said for any man.

◆

As a Senator he has raised the prestige of a chamber where simple integrity and common sense have too often seemed at a premium. He has been a spokesman for all that is best in his party and a staunch supporter of the administration.

◆

There is a man in our midst who is endowed with relentless courage, vision, ability, and profound faith in humanity. At all times he has championed the underdog. If ever for a moment we lose faith in the ability of the nation to find capable leaders under emergency conditions we need only to remember that men like him come forth to give us leadership.

◆

Words are inadequate to describe the qualities of the man I will place in nomination. His record of service to the country equals his devotion to the nation.

I can assure you he possesses all the necessary qualifications—learning, patience, experience, a fine personality, integrity, and, of course, ability. He will serve well, if elected, and bring credit to all his admirers and friends, and great satisfaction to the community.

✦

He is a man of tested ability, sound judgment, and keen perception. He is possessed of a fine character. He is a sincere friend and a devoted worker. These are the attributes which qualify him for the office we are about to fill.

✦

John Jones exemplifies the highest ideals and standards of public service as a career. Modest, painstaking, thorough and devoted to his assigned tasks, his reputation for ability and fairness extend far beyond the borders of this community.

✦

While the offices he occupied all brought honor to him, he, in turn, brought honor to them by the manner in which he filled those offices far above any feeling of partisanship or any political advantage.

✦

He will bring to the office competence, a conscience and an understanding heart.

✦

His rise to his present position is the result of intellect, effort, character and integrity. His career, brief as it is, has already left its mark upon our society.

By his integrity and great learning, he has earned for himself a place of great distinction. He has made an enviable record.

2. *The placing in nomination*

I nominate for president of this organization a distinguished citizen, a peerless leader, Robert Brown.

◆

I deem it a great pleasure to present to you and place in nomination Mr. Robert Brown.

◆

I deem it a personal honor to have the privilege of placing in nomination the name of Robert Brown for reëlection.

◆

I rise to nominate Robert Brown.

◆

The man I place in nomination will follow the example which has been so worthily set by his predecessors. I submit the name of Robert Brown.

◆

My nominee, Robert Brown, will maintain the influence and the standard of this Association and he will discharge all the duties of the office to your satisfaction.

Illustration 1

I have in mind to fill my place, Mr. John Jones. I know him well. He is capable, he is qualified, he is responsible, he is reliable. I speak from experience. I have worked with him for 25 years day in and day out. When he says "yes" he means "yes"; when he says "no" he means "no." He is never on the fence. I feel that he will make an excellent officer. He is my friend, my co-worker, my co-officer. It gives me great pleasure now to nominate him for the position of treasurer.

Illustration 2

I assume that everyone knows whom I will nominate for President of this great organization. I know this man more intimately than any other person in our organization. I have worked with him as closely as two human beings could work together, building the organization, helping him make plans, helping him to create that fine feeling that exists right through our organization today. I have been his assistant, doing whatever I could in every possible manner to make his task easier. You have heard the glowing praise for him from the other speakers. They mentioned his part in the remarkable growth of this organization and the fine leadership that it has enjoyed. Why should I go any further? I nominate for president, John Jones, who is intelligent, an industrious worker, and who possesses a genius for making friends.

Illustration 3

I am not endowed with a great deal of eloquence. Even if I had the skill, I do not believe I could adequately describe the abilities and qualifications of the man

I desire to place in nomination. Such oratorical ability, however, is not necessary for he is well known and appreciated. His services to the Associations and his achievements are common knowledge. I know of no one who has been called upon so often to give service; I know of no one who has given that service as freely as he has. It is a distinct pleasure to place in nomination for the office of president, Brother John Doe.

Illustration 4

The man I am going to place in nomination is known to every active member. He is a friend of the rank and file. His ear and heart are open to all. Nearly everyone has gone to him for guidance and assistance at one time or another. No problem is too small for his thoughtful consideration. For ten years you have elected him to various offices. He has served you well. I deem it a personal honor to place in nomination the name of John Doe for reëlection.

Illustration 5

In order to save time, I nominate for reëlection for the ensuing two years all the incumbent officers to the positions they now hold, and I move they be elected by acclamation.

Illustration 6

I nominate a man who has stood every test. He has measured up to the many responsibilities of his office.

He served his apprenticeship in the junior offices faithfully and his experience now will serve the organization well in these days of stress and strain. It is my pleasure to place in nomination for the office of president, Mr. John Doe.

Illustration 7

Every institution is judged by its elected representatives. This organization has been most fortunate in its officers. They have been loyal men of the very best judgment and of high character. I desire to emphasize the qualities of the man I have nominated. He is able, a man of courage, and loyal to his organization. It is my honor to place before you for the office of president the name of Mr. John Doe.

Illustration 8

I deem it a signal honor to be given the opportunity to submit the name of one of the founders of our Association. He has successfully led our organization for the past few years. He has been a tireless worker and an inspiring leader; he has always been in the top rank of those who have guided us in the performance of our tasks. His colleagues and co-workers have turned to him again and again for advice, for coöperation, for "sacrifice beyond the call of duty"—and never has he failed them. Legwork and brainwork, or just plain hard work—in all of these he has set the example for others to follow. It is because of these qualities, and because he has won the affection and respect of all who know him, that I am privileged to nominate him to succeed himself as president. In reëlecting him we will reward him for his labors for the great cause which has engaged his heart and conscience. I nominate John Jones.

Illustration 9

Yes, words are truly inadequate to describe the qualities of the man I will place in nomination. He possesses all the attributes necessary for the office of secretary. He has worked unceasingly for the betterment of our organization. He has a great capacity for industry. We love him because of his humane attitude and his deep understanding of our problems. He can fill the office as no one else can. Therefore, I present the name of James Jones.

Illustration 10

I nominate for President, Mr. John Doe, a sincere friend, and generous benefactor of our Club. He, more than any one else, is responsible for our beautiful building. Not only did he give money freely but he gave generously of his time, going over every detail of the structure with the architect and the builders. His own good taste is reflected throughout the building. We shall never forget the notable occasion when our building was formally dedicated. It is therefore a cherished privilege for me to be permitted to offer his name for the office of president.

12. Installation Ceremonies, Inaugural Addresses, and Tributes

Installation (Induction) Ceremonies

Examples are given in the pages which follow of rites installing the president, vice-president, secretary and executive board. The ceremony of inducting persons into membership in a union is also given. These forms may be easily converted or adapted to fit similar occasions in other organizations.

Installation (Inaugural) Addresses

The important elements of the installation or inaugural address of an incoming officer are (1) an expression of appreciation for the honor, and (2) a pledge faithfully to perform the duties of the office.

Tributes to Installed Officer

Often one wishes to pay tribute to the person who is installed to office. Such tributes are composed of two elements. The first is praise for the person, and second, good wishes.

Examples of each of the two steps, followed by complete illustrations, are given.

In composing other types of speeches of tribute, this chapter and other chapters of this book will provide an abundance of material.

INSTALLATION (INDUCTION) CEREMONIES

Illustration 1 — Introduction by Chairman

We are gathered here for the purpose of inducting our newly elected president. Many prominent citizens have graced the presidency of this important society. It is a great honor and distinction to become its head. Here we deal not in monetary matters but in protecting the life and liberty of human beings charged with offenses against the law. The office of president of this society requires a man of experience, ability and fortitude, with a knowledge of life, and above all, a heart and mind imbued with a passion for justice. We are fortunate, indeed, that Sam Jones was selected by the membership to this exalted office. By dint of his own energy and ability he has achieved a notable career, and by sacrifice and devotion he has attained a reputation of being one of the most charitable and civic-minded citizens of our community. Small wonder then that so many people have gathered here to pay him tribute. We extend to him a hearty welcome. I predict that he too will become one of our great presidents. I am mindful of the fact that the chairman is not expected to make a lengthy speech so I will proceed at once to the business before us and call on the distinguished personages who have come here to honor him.

Illustration 2 — President (Fraternal)

It is now my function, as it is my privilege and pleasure, to induct our new president into office. As I hand you the emblem of office as president, it is a great satisfaction to me to welcome you as my successor. You are in every way worthy of the honor conferred upon you tonight. For many years you have served us ably and well. I am sure that you have the same great love for our fraternity that I have. I know that the leadership which you now assume is in very safe and capable hands. And now, with my best wishes and every confidence in your success, I turn over to you the presidency and the leadership of our order. May I leave this closing thought with you: "Nothing succeeds like successors."

Illustration 3 — President (Union)

Brother Jones, you have been chosen to preside over the destinies of Local 234 for the next two years. The president's first duty is to lead the local to success and prosperity. Upon your skill and ability depend its honor, reputation, and usefulness. It will be your especial duty to preserve its reputation and dignity. You are to permit nothing to tarnish its excellent reputation. It is your duty to remind the members of the fine traditions of our union, of the sacrifices made that they may enjoy the prevailing terms and conditions of employment. You should be as careful of the reputation of our local as you would of that of your family. It is also your duty and no doubt it will be your pleasure to teach our members to be good unionists, sober, industrious, and to do all things to be a credit to it. A president's paramount duty is to preserve peace and harmony—a matter on which no specific instructions can be given.

The powers you possess are extraordinary powers. You have powers that the presiding officer of no other organization has. You are admonished not to exercise that power in an arbitrary or dictatorial manner, but with a determination to administer impartial justice to the end that peace and harmony may be preserved. The president whose rule is just and fair will gain respect and support even from those who do not agree with him. When necessary, however, authority should be used fearlessly and firmly. The president has a duty to those who follow him to hand down the office with its dignity, its rights, its privileges and its responsibilities unchanged. I will now administer the oath of office: "Do you solemnly promise that you will serve the union as president for the next two years and will perform all the duties appertaining to that office to the best of your ability?"

Illustration 4 — Vice-President

The International Constitution states that the vice-president is to perform all the duties of the president in his absence and to take the chair whenever he requests. You have heard me describe the powers and responsibilities of the president. Those powers and responsibilities are also yours. (Administers oath.)

Illustration 5 — Secretary (Fraternal)

The secretary's duties are substantially of a business character, and are of the highest importance to the welfare of the lodge. Punctuality in attendance at the meetings of the lodge is an indispensable requisite of the secretary. He should be first in his place at its meetings, and the nature of his duties is such that he can scarcely avoid being the last to leave the lodge room. He is particularly charged with the duty of watching the proceedings of the lodge and making a complete record of all things proper to be written; to keep the financial accounts between the lodge and its members; to receive all moneys due to the lodge and pay them into the hands of the treasurer; to prepare the annual reports for the Grand Lodge; to have in charge the seal of the lodge, and to perform all other duties pertaining to the office, as may be ordered by the presidents.

Illustration 6 — Secretary (Union)

The skillful performance of your duties are of the highest importance to the welfare of the union and its members. The qualities which distinguish a good secretary are quick comprehension, prompt attention to business, sterling integrity in all his dealings with the union and its members. Your records as secretary constitute the current history of the events of the union. The records you prepare will be conveyed to future generations and will be the monument by which your work will be remembered. Your own honor and the confidence the members repose in you will arouse you to that faithfulness in the discharge of the duties of your office which its important nature demands. The office of the secretary is the most responsible and important office that the members of this union can confer upon a man. It should be given only to men of the strictest integrity. But once a union has a true and trusted secretary, it should not dispense with his services, but continue to elect him as long as he can be prevailed upon to serve. A union which has secured for this office a man who is as interested in his work as you are will do well to value him highly and retain him in the office until he grows gray in the service. (Administers oath.)

Illustration 7 — Executive Board

Each of you has been elected by the membership to serve two years on the all important executive board.

The responsibility of the executive board cannot be overstated. In the last analysis it is you who make or break a union's efficiency. The executive board is often the court of last resort. You are the court which decides grievances. Every member of the executive board should make a determined effort to gain a reputation for fair dealing. You must try to see the point of view of the member who is being judged by you. Consider each case on its merits. Be willing to accept the logical conclusion flowing from the facts even if it involves some concession on your part. Keep an open mind and listen to both sides. (Administers oath.)

Illustration 8 — Union members

We have been joined together since 19___ to build a strong union, to improve conditions, to obtain better working conditions. Great sacrifices were made by our members to realize these aims. The rise of our union has often been compared to the rise of our nation. Every American is acquainted with the story of how thirteen weak colonies won their freedom from the English kings by organizing themselves into a union of states. As it was then, so it is true with us. Hundreds of workers, who were weak by themselves, united to get rid of the sweatshop. These hundreds laid the foundation of our union. But just as the thirteen states—once they won their freedom—grew to forty-eight powerful states composing the greatest nation on earth, so our little union has grown in membership, in prestige, and respect. Our members now enjoy many rights. They cannot be discharged at will. They are guaranteed sanitary conditions, minimum wages, maximum hours, vacations with pay, welfare funds, insurance, sick and health benefits.

Now that you have heard what the union is and does, it is up to you to decide whether you wish to be a member and whether you wish to assume the responsibilities which union membership carries with it. If you so decide, you may take the pledge. Before reading the pledge, I should like to know whether you have any questions. There being none, will you please repeat after me: "I, John Doe, do hereby solemnly and sincerely pledge to obey the laws of the International Union and Local 234 to the best of my ability and to bear true allegiance to my local." You are now members of the union. You will be presented with a copy of our union constitution. Read it; know it; let it be your guide.

INSTALLATION (INAUGURAL) ADDRESSES

1. Appreciation

The honor that has been conferred upon me is a great one. That I should have been thought worthy of this high distinction arouses in me mixed emotions of humility and profound gratitude.

◆

I am sure you realize that I am grateful to you for this honor. I have a sense of my inadequacy to preside over this great organization, but I will do my utmost to justify your faith in me.

◆

This new distinction which is about to be conferred upon me brings up a sense of pride and humility. I renew my resolution to try to merit the confidence which has been reposed in me.

I devoutly hope that I will justify the confidence reposed in me by the Mayor, the political party which nominated me, and the voters who elected me.

✦

I realize the grave duties and responsibilities of the high office to which I have been elected. I enter upon my duties with a sense of humility, with an awareness of the attendant obligations, and with anxiety lest my abilities fail to keep pace with my eagerness to render the service you expect.

✦

To take the oath of office as president is always a solemn occasion. The responsibility of directing the affairs of this great order is never to be lightly undertaken. I am fully aware of the magnitude of the responsibilities of this office. I am alert to the duty I owe the members of this proud organization.

✦

I am so pleased with it all that my cup of happiness is filled to overflowing. This day will remain in my memory forever, brightening every dark moment and lifting any shadow that may cross my path.

✦

May I tell you how grateful I am for bestowing this honor upon me? Your loyalty and faith in me will be my greatest assets in the administration of my new office.

✦

The enthusiastic support which has come from the membership has been inspiring and a stimulant to me.

1 extend to them, my heartfelt thanks for this highest honor in their power to grant.

◆

Let me say without hesitation that I accept this great honor. I accept it with pride and gratitude and a full heart. Most of all I thank you for the confidence you express in me. Today, I thank you in words. After to-day, I hope to translate my appreciation into deeds and conduct.

◆

I am indeed as humble as I am proud of your decision to confer upon me the leadership of this organization. To those who have worked so hard to make this occa-sion a success I extend my thanks. Your kindness and the warmth of your friendship will not be forgotten. It is great to know you and to work with you. Thank you again.

2. Pledge faithfully to perform the duties of office

I pledge my best efforts as your president to continue the glorious work of our organization. I know I can count on your support and coöperation. With it, I can-not fail.

◆

In this staggering task you have given me I shall always try "to love justice, to do mercy and walk humbly with my God." In the language of my oath of office and in conformity with the spirit of that oath, "I will faithfully discharge my duties to the best of my ability." My every effort will be exerted to justify the expressions of praise and confidence uttered here tonight.

✦

With the help of the Divine Creator, I shall strive to be a capable, conscientious and humble presiding officer.

✦

I will be faithful in the discharge of my duties. I will be courteous and considerate of all. I am fully aware of the duty I owe to the membership and shall discharge that duty to the best of my abilities.

✦

I recognize clearly the weight of the responsibility that you have placed upon me and I assure you that I shall never give short weight to those responsibilities.

✦

I am grateful to you for the confidence which you have in me and I pledge to give to you and to all the members the best that is in me.

✦

I solemnly promise the members that my devotion is to them and only to them. I will try to justify the confidence they have placed in me.

Illustration 1

To all my friends I wish to express my gratitude and thanks for having taken time out to come here, and for the good wishes so many of you have sent to me. I took the oath of office to carry out, to the best of my ability, the duties of president of this great organization. I shall

endeavor to do this with, I trust, the assistance and coöperation of my friends and the members of this organization. Once again, I thank you all.

Illustration 2

I assure you that I am touched by your demonstration
of confidence, and feel very deeply the responsibilities
that rest upon me in this position. These are very trying
days, days when all the qualities of constructive leadership are put to a severe test. Therefore, I am under no
illusions. While I am very happy over this wonderful
expression of confidence, I realize that the work of the
ensuing year is going to be increasingly difficult. I renew
all promises I made the first time I was elected to this
high office. I will apply myself, God willing, to the task
and do the best I can.

Illustration 3

Let my first words be those of gratitude to all of you
for having elected me as your president. This is a great
association and it is a great honor to be its president. But
I am very humble when I think of my illustrious predecessors. The power and prestige which it now enjoys
reflect so greatly the loyalty and the devotion of their
great talents to its cause. Yet, I have complete confidence,
despite my own limitations, that this administration will
measure up and will carry forward the banner of this
association.

Illustration 4

It is not my purpose at this hour to weary you with a long speech. It would be a poor return for the great kindness which you have shown in selecting me as your president. It is an honor that I greatly prize and my only regret is that I may not be able to follow the splendid example of my predecessor—a man who with distinction and success has administered and watched over the affairs of this association during the past year. He has administered its affairs in a way that has made it a subject of regret that he could not be persuaded to continue for another term. It is my distinct privilege to pay him this tribute of friendship. It is a great privilege that you have conferred upon me. Not only because you have selected me as your president, an honor which I cherish greatly, but because my selection has afforded me this opportunity of expressing my respect and admiration for the guest of honor. For your kindness in selecting me as your president for the coming year, from my heart, I thank you.

Illustration 5

I am very happy to be here today surrounded by my family, my colleagues, my co-officers and by the president of the Grand Lodge who has just sworn me in. I want you all to know I am deeply grateful that you are here today. I shall at all times do my level best to justify the confidence you have reposed in me.

Illustration 6

This is the first opportunity I have had to thank you for the very great honor which you have conferred upon me. In this distinguished audience, I take upon myself in all sincerity the obligation to discharge the duties incumbent upon the president of this association to the best of my ability. I know that I shall have your coöperation without asking for it. I hope that we may carry on during the coming year and that we shall all work together for the greater prestige of our association.

Illustration 7

To you, I trust, this has been an impressive ceremony. To me, as you probably realize, it has been doubly so and almost overwhelming. I am especially grateful to the membership for electing me to this high post. I will endeavor as best I can to carry on the position of president in such a manner that the confidence reposed in me by the membership will be justified.

The praise has been overwhelming and overgenerous but after it has been sufficiently discounted it has nevertheless been music to my ears. To all my friends I wish to express my gratification and thanks for having taken time out to come here and for the good wishes so many of you have sent to me.

Illustration 8

You have placed an obligation upon my shoulders and at the same time imposed a trust upon me. The obligation is welcome. The trust, I assure you, will be fulfilled. I want to thank the members for the great honor of electing me to the high office and to my friend, our outgoing leader, for administering the oath of office to me. I thank the officers for many acts of kindness, consideration and helpfulness which they have extended to me since my election. I hope I may continue to receive the benefit of their experience and wisdom.

Illustration 9

I am mindful of all the duties and obligations that go with this office. I would accept it with great misgivings except that I am assured that I am, for a time, to be captain of a ship in which every member of the crew is capable of being captain and in which there is a spirit of coöperation that makes holding office easy and pleasant. Relying on that spirit, I have accepted this position, and it shall be my earnest endeavor while I am captain of the ship to hold it on that fine course which was so ably chartered and so faithfully followed by all my predecessors.

TRIBUTES TO INSTALLED OFFICER

1. Praise for the person honored

Your appointment is cause for deep satisfaction because the office is one of national distinction. The society is to be congratulated upon obtaining the services of so able a man as you are. Your accomplishments and career have left an imprint upon the people of our community whom you have served so faithfully for many years.

✦

He is a great American with faith in the American people and in the democratic processes. His convictions and faith show through everything he has said and has written.

✦

Your distinctive attributes have brought you signal honors as you reach another milestone in life's journey.

✦

You can take pride in the fact that your faithful performance of an exacting and vital duty has contributed much in maintaining the people's respect for our government.

✦

You have the artist's sensitivity to people and situations. You seem to know instinctively how people think and feel and your personality reacts automatically to every change in the atmosphere.

✦

Genial, companionable and cultured, you have endeared yourself to all with whom you have come in contact.

✦

No one in this community exceeds you in the possession of integrity and ability. You are proof that unassuming, able and conscientious public service does attain, at times, its just reward.

You are a true, selfless citizen and a loyal public officer. Your sense of honor and your integrity are qualities which we should all try to emulate.

✦

You are scrupulous, fair and impartial. You are gentle, understanding and considerate. You embrace the principle that loyalty runs in two directions.

✦

The appointment of a man of your attainments is the best assurance that the task will be capably performed. Your acceptance of this post may well be hailed with satisfaction.

✦

You have the rare quality of being able to unite all who work with you into a cohesive unit. This is because you have taken the time to know personally and closely all with whom you have been associated.

✦

I rejoice with you on this wonderful opportunity that has come to you to serve your community.

✦

You have established yourself as a friend of the underprivileged. Your humane philosophy, your capacity for understanding, and your tireless efforts on behalf of those less fortunate are the qualities which endear you to all. You rank very high, indeed, among the friends of the needy.

✦

It is impossible to translate into words the respect and admiration for you that I see etched upon the faces of your friends assembled here to pay you homage.

As you would expect of a man of his breadth of interests, he has been active in all manner of fraternal, civic and philanthropic organizations; so many that I wouldn't attempt to detail them to you.

2. Good wishes

As one of the many in whom you evoke admiration and respect, I take this occasion to wish you every happiness.

✦

In concluding, I want to do my bit to give you a good, big, hearty send-off and to wish you well.

✦

I need hardly express the hope that this will be a stepping stone to even greater honors in the future.

✦

I hope that you will derive from your work the satisfaction that comes to a man from the knowledge that he is serving mankind.

✦

We hope that God's grace will accompany you throughout the remainder of your life and that He may grant you peace and enjoyment.

✦

It is my sincere wish that the relinquishment of the cares which you have borne so faithfully will result in your improved health.

✦

We hope you may live to a ripe old age so that you may enjoy the companionship and society of your family and the satisfaction of knowing that yours was a job well done.

✦

I hope that the future will bring you everything that you could wish.

✦

We wish you good luck and happiness in your new position.

✦

I have every confidence that you will be eminently successful in any enterprise you undertake. God bless you and may you continue to enjoy life at its best.

Illustration 1 — To installed officer

You have demonstrated your ability for leadership; you have shown great industry in your work and eloquence in the meeting room. Your most important quality, however, is your absolute fairness. No man who has ascended to the presidency of this organization has enjoyed a finer reputation than is yours. The membership has deep respect and warm affection for you. On behalf of your co-officers, I congratulate you and wish you long life, happiness, and continued successes.

Illustration 2 — To installed officer

You are exceedingly well equipped for the high office you are about to assume. You are an industrious worker. Your sterling character, great ability, and high integrity are our assurances that you will carry on in the finest traditions of our order. I have no doubt that you, who are possessed of such fine attributes of mind and heart, will enjoy a long, happy and successful career, and that you will be a credit to the organization, to your friends, and to yourself. To me has been assigned the pleasant task of administering to you the oath of office. Please repeat after me: "I solemnly and sincerely promise and swear that I will serve the organization as president for the next two years and will perform all the duties appertaining to that office to the best of my ability." I congratulate you and now pronounce you the president of our organization.

Illustration 3 — To installed officer

This is rightfully an occasion for celebration. It is difficult for me to say what is in my mind and heart without repeating, because everything has already been well said. The privilege of greeting you as our new president thrills me. You have made an enviable record and have won the confidence of the members. You have earned the privilege of leading them for the next two years. My best wishes to you for a successful administration.

Illustration 4 — To installed officer

We, your junior officers, rejoice with you in the fact that you have been chosen for the responsibility of this high office. We know that your judgment, experience, and energy will guide you successfully through the years of your presidency. We pledge ourselves to work in harmony with you to the fullest extent. We cannot think of a more vital message than this: "Go forward with strength and conviction to help you fulfill our highest destiny."

13. Retirement Addresses and Tributes

A retiring officer, such as the president of a club, generally expresses his thanks to the organization and his associates for their support and assistance in carrying out the duties of his office. He begins by expressing appreciation for the honor of serving and the support he has received, and he concludes by offering good wishes to his successor.

The speeches which follow illustrate the ideas presented in this preface.

The farewell speech, is a speech of tribute to the outgoing or retiring officer, follows a similar pattern that is, appreciation for the person who is retiring and good wishes for the future.

1. *Appreciation*

I have stated many times, both publicly and privately, my high regard for the members and my colleagues. I have learned to admire them for their personal qualities and have appreciated the splendid fashion in which they coöperated with me in the performance of my tasks. Nor am I unmindful of their unfailing courtesy at all times and of their loyalty to me.

◆

I want to tell you of my deep appreciation for the wise counsel and unwavering support I have received from you and for your great sacrifice of time and energy.

◆

I am deeply grateful to the membership and to my associates for the confidence which they have placed in me and I pledge myself to give to my distinguished successor, the best that is in me.

◆

I have received your generous support of every part of my program and I, in turn, pledge to my successor who has been a tireless and unselfish worker for the organization, my whole-hearted support and coöperation in the administration of this important position.

◆

I want to express to the members my great appreciation for the coöperation they have given me as president.

◆

May I tell you how grateful I am for your unselfish help during my term? Your faith and loyalty were my

greatest assets. I hope I may continue to come to you
for inspiration.

✦

I want you to know how greatly I appreciate the
splendid support and coöperation which have been given
me during my tenure as chairman.

✦

I am grateful to my fellow officers for their confidence
in me in the past and particularly during the current
year when they were confronted with an issue concern-
ing me personally.

✦

The enthusiastic support with which the members
have favored me has been an inspiration and a great comfort. I extend to the membership my heartfelt thanks
for their loyal support.

2. *Good wishes to successor*

To my mind you are the greatest leader the organization has had and my admiration and respect will always
be yours. You can count on my all-out coöperation.

✦

It will be a privilege to serve this organization under
your inspiring leadership. I have supported and endorsed
all your proposals and will continue to do so.

✦

I wish you a successful administration and express the

hope that, should you find that I can be helpful at some time in the future, you will not hesitate to call upon me.

✦

I pledge my fullest coöperation to the new president and his administration. We will make a united effort to meet the present problems facing the organization by the most effective means.

✦

I know you will supply the necessary inspiration and enthusiasm to carry our aims into effect and that your administration will go down as one of the most successful.

✦

I congratulate you and hope that your tenure of office will be happy and successful.

✦

I heartily approve of your program. You are deserving of the highest praise, and will have our consistent support.

Illustration 1 — Retirement Addresses

I can hardly realize that four years have passed since I first appeared before you to take my oath of office as president of this organization. The intervening years have been full and difficult. Busy as they were and great as have been the burdens, I enjoyed my years as president and I am grateful for the friends I have made here. I am particularly indebted to that loyal body of members who have worked so faithfully with me. Their confidence and support made my task easier.

My illustrious successor can count on my whole-hearted coöperation during the four years that lie ahead of him. He is one of the sweetest-natured and most even-tempered men in the organization. It will be a joy to work with him. I know he will give of his real ability, freely, graciously and to the fullest possible degree. He deserves our coöperation.

Illustration 2

I want to express to you, the members of our organization, my great appreciation for the coöperation which you have given me as president. Your support has not been passive or mere approval; it has been spontaneous, active and enthusiastic. You have been loyal and unswerving in your support. I am very grateful. Many of you have willingly accepted difficult committee assignments. Many of you have taken time out from your vocations to render services to the organization at great personal sacrifice and some financial loss. As for my personal staff, no one could have had a more loyal and hardworking one and their devotion to me I shall never forget. The tributes that have come to me are not fully deserved. Nevertheless, it is gratifying to receive this recognition. I trust you will give to my successor that same degree of coöperation you have given me. You are a grand group of men and to each of you I owe my affection, gratitude and respect. God bless you and carry on.

Illustration 3

Two years ago I stood here your newly-elected president and stated that I was fully aware of my own limitations and had no intention of competing with any of my great predecessors in office. I expressed complete confidence that the administration then starting and now ending would fully measure up to our high standards. I based that confidence upon the assistance I was certain would come from the former presidents, the officers, the committees, and above all from the membership. My confidence has been fully justified. Thanks to all, the years have recorded a steady rise in the power and prestige of this association. Each month has been marked by a steady and healthy rise in our membership.

Now I come to the end of the road. The friendly coöperation and the warm comradeship of all of you have dispelled the difficulties; the path proved a pleasant one, and the two years, for me, were memorable and happy. You have answered promptly and wholeheartedly every call I made upon you for service. The two years have heartened me with their enriching experiences. They have brought me many new and wonderful friendships which are now among my most cherished possessions. My heartfelt thanks then to all of my fellow members as I step back into the ranks to serve under one whose record of accomplishments ensures us that under his leadership our beloved association will go forward to greater achievements.

Illustration 4

The many kind words which have been said of me on the occasion of my retirement, make me blush with embarrassment. I could not, without vanity, assume that I merit such praise though I cannot deny that I have tried to discharge my duties to the best of my ability. I can only thank you all for these expressions of your belief that I have made some approach to the ideal of a good president. I am profoundly grateful to the members who helped me to serve them. It is literally true that my service has been a labor of love. Our choice for president for the ensuing two years can, of course, count on our coöperation. In spite of the many demands upon his time, the welfare of the society has always been his prime concern. He deserves all the help we can give.

Illustration 5

It becomes my duty to turn over the emblem of my office to my distinguished successor. I have greatly enjoyed this period of service and have prized the privilege of trying in some way to add to the effectiveness of this organization. The incoming president is one who has long labored as chairman of one of the most important of our committees. His contribution to the organization has been so great I am sure the organization has enhanced its own importance by selecting him as its next president. I venture to say that no one among the members has given more lavishly of his time than has the gentleman who will now take the gavel as president of our organization.

Illustration 6

It is our custom at this stage of the dinner for the retiring president to hand the gavel to his successor in order that the new president may entertain and put the motion to adjourn. We are most fortunate today in electing as the president for the coming year a man of wide experience and great ability. We are assured of a great president. He is also a man of so kind and lovable a nature that it will be a joy all through the year to have him preside over our meetings. I have the greatest pleasure now in handing this gavel to John Jones.

Illustration 7 — Tributes to Retiring Official

I will avail myself of the opportunity to refer briefly to the purpose of this event. We are here as friends and associates of John Doe to express our good wishes and affection for him. John has just completed 25 years of service to our organization. During that time he labored unceasingly as our secretary and has earned surcease from his duties. It is proper that we pay him these tributes he is about to receive. I am pleased to introduce the speakers who will honor him and give him a good start on the road to retirement.

Illustration 8

We are sorry to learn of your impending retirement. You have been a sturdy fixture of our organization in one office or another for many years. You have been a decided credit to us. The many fine tributes which were paid to you are an inspiring manifestation of the high esteem in which you are held. I want to supplement them by adding a personal expression of deep regard for you. Your unfailing courtesy, the high fidelity with which you performed the most difficult tasks, and your great sacrifices on behalf of our organization more than justify all the nice things which have been said about you. God bless you and may you continue to enjoy life at its best.

Illustration 9

Your decision to retire as vice-president has been received by us with deep regret. I regard your retirement as a personal loss. The ties of nearly 20 years are not easily broken. For a man of your vigor and devotion to duty, I know this decision was a difficult one to make. However, you have the satisfaction of knowing that everything you undertook was ably and conscientiously performed. Your service as vice-president has covered a good part of the history of this organization. You participated in planning policies which have more than doubled its membership, increased its efficiency and its prestige. Your faithfulness in attending and participating in the meetings of the Executive Board has not gone unnoticed. My own work as president has benefited from the example and counsel derived from your seniority in years and experience. For that I thank you. It is my earnest wish that the relinquishment of the cares which you have borne so faithfully will result in your improved health. Our selfish feeling of personal loss is tempered by the hope and belief that the change will result in your physical betterment. Therefore, we say: Farewell; we'll miss you. May God bless you and prosper you!

Illustration 10

It is with genuine regret that I feel I must, for the personal reasons you gave, accept your resignation. The loyal service you rendered, the understanding you have shown of all our complex problems, the wise counsel you gave in seeking their solution, make your leaving a sad blow indeed. All the members of our organization, who know the quality and importance of these services, will share my feelings. Few of them, however, can realize the great courage and devotion you have shown in sticking to your post in the face of such compelling reasons of health. They will, I know, share with me the fervent wish for your speedy and complete recovery. It is my earnest hope that I may at some early date call upon you once again to help meet our organization's needs.

Illustration 11

With heartfelt regret and great reluctance, we see you relinquishing the symbol of your office as president of this association. I know how difficult have been the problems to which you fell heir when you took office. With all these problems you have dealt with rare tact and judgment. For all you have done you have earned the thanks of every member. Our regret at your leaving us, before the expiration of your term, is tempered, however, with the proud consciousness that you are soon to assume national responsibilities. I give you the assurance of your brethren that you take with you their entire confidence, their good wishes and their affection.

Illustration 12

Brother Easton, you have been a pillar of the fraternity in one office or another for the past 25 years. On December 31st you will have completed 25 years of service. As everyone here knows, you are a modest individual, very exact in the performance of your duties, a fine personality and a wonderful man. It is regrettable that illness now compels a retreat from fraternal activities. After 25 years of service to us you retire to the quietude of private life. May retirement bring back to you good health and may you enjoy happiness for many years. In saying farewell it is with the hope that it will not be good-bye but au revoir, and that you will come around to see us every time you get a chance.

14. Closing Remarks

As the chairman your function is not concluded until you have adjourned the meeting. You should express thanks for the interest and coöperation of the audience and bid them a cordial farewell. Be brief because the listeners will be making for the exits.

(Parliamentary Procedure: During a formal meeting when discussions are completed it is then proper to adjourn. Any member may rise and say, "Mr. President, I move we adjourn." The motion must be seconded. Then it is stated by the president and voted upon just as any other motion is. The chairman may say, "If there is no objection, the meeting stands adjourned.")

Illustration 1

I will conclude by wishing you good luck and saying Godspeed to all of you. But first I want to thank the chairman of the program committee for the thoughtful and splendid program which he projected and planned. And may I close this meeting with words which, in many languages, in many forms, in many religions, have brought comfort and strength. "May the peace of God, which passeth all understanding, be with us and remain with us always."

Illustration 2

We have come to the closing moments of the program and it falls to the president to say the last words of farewell. May I begin by expressing the deepest appreciation of which I am capable for the trust which has been reposed in me in selecting me to serve as your presiding officer. I have tried to justify your trust. I want to thank you all for coming here and I hope we will have the pleasure of seeing you again. Thank you.

Illustration 3

I ask that we now conclude these memorial exercises by rising for a moment of silent tribute to the memory of our beloved brother.

Illustration 4

I regret that we must conclude this discussion. Thank

you for the interesting and illuminating contributions you have made to our understanding of a most complex issue.

Illustration 5

I think everything that should be said or could be said on this occasion has been ably stated. I am not going to protract these proceedings any further by what would amount to mere recapitulation.

Illustration 6

I now declare this most interesting and inspiring meeting adjourned.

Illustration 7

I regret to say that the time has now come when we must conclude this discussion. Therefore, this discussion is now concluded with renewed thanks to our distinguished speakers.

Illustration 8

The hour is late and you have been most patient, kind and generous. The delay in beginning this ceremony was due to circumstances over which, I assure you, we had no control, and that increases my appreciation and my gratitude for your patience in having remained until now.

Illustration 9

In bringing this meeting to a close, it is with the feeling that much of a constructive nature has been accomplished, and I wish to thank the membership and the officers for making this possible.

Illustration 10

Our meeting has been a fruitful one. I believe we can all go to our homes secure in the knowledge of a job well done. Thank you and good night.

Illustration 11

In closing I want to thank the past presidents without whose inspiration our project, so satisfactorily accomplished, would not have been begun.

Illustration 12

I am advised that all of the business of this convention having been dispatched, my only function as your new president is to entertain and put the motion that this convention now adjourn.

Illustration 13

I now declare this very successful, useful and interesting meeting adjourned.

15. Congratulatory Messages

A message of felicitations and congratulations has three elements, (1) the offer of congratulations, (2) praise for the person, and (3) best wishes for success.

However, in telegrams, where brevity is desirable, not all of these characteristics need be given.

Material and samples of congratulatory messages are furnished in this chapter. If the form does not exactly fit the situation, it can be easily adapted or altered.

1. Offer of congratulations

I offer you my most sincere congratulations upon your success at the polls.

✦

May I add my felicitations to the many you have already received on your election.

✦

I am happy for this opportunity to add my voice to the chorus of congratulations.

✦

The 25th anniversary provides us with an opportunity to extend our warmest congratulations to your organization and its membership on its splendid accomplishments.

✦

I congratulate you warmly on this happy and memorable occasion.

✦

I could not let so memorable an event pass without sending you my hearty congratulations.

✦

I congratulate you and the members of your Association on the wise choice they have made in selecting you to lead them.

2. Praise

There are few men for whom I have the same deep affection and respect that I have for you. You are in every sense a leader of men and an ideal administrator. I am happy to be included among your friends. I am privileged to join the hundreds who on this occasion are paying you small homage, indeed, compared to your outstanding contributions.

◆

Your election is an inspiring manifestation of the high esteem in which you are held.

◆

This recognition is most appropriate in view of your many contributions to the progress of the lodge.

◆

This honor is well earned. It is not only a compliment for the past but reflects upon the future.

◆

This was a unique opportunity to reëlect to the leadership of your fine order one of the most sterling personalities in it. John Doe's wisdom and lofty idealism, combined with his vigor and unequaled experience, will be a tower of strength to you at a time when they are very much needed.

◆

Under your wise, fearless, and strong-hearted leadership the organization will increase in membership and influence.

◆

The excellent work done by you during the past many years clearly warrants this testimonial dinner. The strength and recognition attained by the organization during those years are a silent tribute to your able efforts.

3. Best wishes for success

We hope that you will enjoy a long, happy and successful administration.

✦

Sincere best wishes to you for a successful administration. May you continue to enjoy splendid health.

✦

My best wishes to you for the success of your campaign and for the wonderful work you plan to do.

✦

I hope that, no matter what the future holds for you, God will always shower upon you his choicest blessings.

✦

May Almighty God give you strength and wisdom to fulfill your responsibilities during the next four years.

✦

May you be blessed with good health for many years to come, so that you may continue to give your services to the people of this community.

✦

I pray and earnestly hope that the time is not far off when you will go on to even greater honors.

✦

We rejoice in the recognition which has been accorded to you by this community. We pray that God may grant you the years and health to pursue your arduous duties.

✦

We join with your many friends in renewed assurances of our own high regard.

I wish you well in the years ahead. I remind you that you follow in the footsteps of fine men who have gone from this school and have won well deserved public recognition and acclaim. You have a rich heritage. Preserve it well.

◆

May we have the benefit of your good health, happiness and leadership for many years to come.

◆

We hope that your tenure will be happy and healthful. Your colleagues will do everything to make it a very pleasant one for you.

◆

May the Sutton Association continue to carry on with vigor and effectiveness and may its first twenty years be but a mere beginning of its great service to the life of the Community.

◆

May I offer you my complete support and coöperation in this most important election. I know that the community will rally to your support.

Illustration 1

I congratulate you and wish you long life, good health and happiness. You have earned the gratitude of men and women throughout the City as a great leader in the fight for human decency and honesty in government. Under your inspired leadership I am sure the needs of the City for better housing and fuller employment will be met.

My best wishes for the success of your forward-looking program.

Illustration 2

Warmest congratulations to you upon your election as President. All of us in the association have good reason to be proud of the success you have attained. Sincere best wishes for a successful administration.

Illustration 3

May I add my felicitations to the many you have already received on your election to the Presidency. I think the members of your organization should also be congratulated upon their choice. I know you will be a credit to those who sponsored you. Best wishes for a successful administration.

Illustration 4

I congratulate you upon your appointment. You have always displayed an enlightened policy toward all city employes. You have mediated successfully scores of labor difficulties which otherwise would have resulted in the loss of wages to many workers. You have given the city an honest administration. I hope you will receive the recognition your brilliant skill deserves.

Illustration 5

The people of this City are fortunate to have elected

you as its representative. Your liberal and humane outlook on the problems of our times and your courage and ability to do something about them, assures a successful administration. Congratulations and may you continue to receive ever greater rewards and recognition.

Illustration 6

After another election under our free, democratic form of government, the people of our City have voted to continue you in office. I congratulate you. May Almighty God give you good health to fulfill the obligations of your office.

Illustration 7

Your appointment deserves unreserved approval and congratulations. Your eminence in the community, your stature as a lawyer, and your notable experience in public life all assure a continuing contribution. This is the sort of appointment that inspires confidence in the courts. The quality of the judiciary depends on the standard of selection. We can depend upon you to make an addition that will be widely felt to the general benefit.

Illustration 8

On behalf of my associates and myself, I wish to express our felicitations and congratulations upon your appointment. When the vacancy occurred a few months ago, we were glad to see that the appointment went to you. We join in wishing you a long and successful career in this most important office. I wish to add that from ~vhat we have seen of your work since you came here on a ~emporary basis, we are certain that you will discharge the duties of your office well and faithfully, and without fear or favor, and that you will do equal justice to the poor and to the rich.

16. Greetings

Greetings for special events are written usually for publication in the magazine or newspaper of an organization. In this chapter are illustrative greetings for the following occasions and holidays:

Anniversary of organization
Anniversary of magazine
Birthday
Christmas
New Year
Passover
Thanksgiving Day

Illustration 1 — Anniversary of Organization

On the occasion of the anniversary we are celebrating, I wish to extend my greetings to the members whose support and coöperation have made it possible for the leadership to achieve so many notable successes. While our organization enjoys the respect of others, we don't intend to rest on our laurels. We are the first ones to recognize that perfection does not exist and that there is always room for improvement. We are aware that much is yet to be done, and that we cannot afford to remain inert. We must either go forward or backward. It isn't like us to go backward. A progressive organization must look to the future, more than to the past but, lest we forget, from time to time it is also important that we review our achievements and the failures of the past.

Illustration 2 — Anniversary of Magazine

On your 25th birthday a friendly salute, a warm typewriter toast. Through your example of accuracy, honesty and fairness, your magazine has exerted a great influence on the community. Your enterprise, ability, integrity and adherence to the principles of sound journalism are an inspiration to all reputable periodicals. Your courageous stand for truth has long been a fountainhead from which our community has derived nourishment and vigor in its fight for liberty and justice.

Illustration 3 — Birthday

As you celebrate your birthday I look anew, and with ever increasing admiration, upon your distinguished career. Few men in our organization have been privileged to serve in so many important capacities as you have and certainly none has done so with such brilliance and devotion. The officers and members of your organization are proud of you; they know you have used your great talents in the interest of all. May you have many more years of happiness and health and may we continue to have the benefit of your counsel and judgment.

Illustration 4 — Christmas

The spirit of Christmas is in the air. Christmas never fails to bring to mind the divine words "Peace on earth and good will towards men." So, on this Christmas Day, while we exchange good wishes and entertain visions of a better future for us and for everyone else, we solemnly dedicate ourselves to do whatever is in our power for the realization of "peace on earth and good will towards men." Within a few days our entire staff will be at their cheery firesides to spend the holidays with their families. Of the 365 days which constitute a year, none is so heart-warming as Christmas. This year we promise again, as in the past, to drink a toast on Christmas Day to our entire force which shouldered the burdens of the organization throughout the year. We can only conclude by wishing you and yours the Merriest Christmas.

Illustration 5 — Christmas

As we draw near the most joyous season of the year, I offer you our sincerest wishes for a most enjoyable holiday and our warmest and kindest congratulations. May the years which lie ahead bring you deep satisfaction and happiness in your accomplishments. A Merry Christmas to you and to those near and dear to you.

Illustration 6 — New Year

May I extend to you and your family best wishes for a very happy, healthy and prosperous New Year. With another milepost in sight and another year beckoning us with hopes and opportunities for service, we stop a moment to reflect upon our pleasant relations of the year about to close. It is, indeed, with gratitude that I look back upon the past year and thank you for your support and trust in electing me your president. And now at the very outset of the New Year, I appeal to you to attend the meetings. Your presence will be the barometer for our efforts. It will spur the administration on to greater achievements. It will be more than an indication of support; it will be an inspiration for even better programs.

Illustration 7 — Passover

It is again my privilege as Mayor to extend warmest greetings to all my fellow citizens of the Jewish faith on the occasion of the wondrous festival of Passover. As you celebrate your people's emancipation from slavery and their exodus from Egypt—which for 4,000 years has been your inspiration against the forces of evil and tyranny—may you be strengthened in your resolve to preserve the hallowed ideals of the Passover—liberation and freedom. The story of Passover is as fresh and appealing today as when it was first told in ancient times, and its message of freedom is no less moving and significant; for the struggle against tyranny and oppression, which Passover commemorates, is as old as the ruins of the Pharoahs and as new as the latest newspaper headline.

Illustration 8 — Thanksgiving Greetings

With so many other weeks in the year devoted to commercial or charitable purposes, it is good to have a week set aside for giving thanks. Thanksgiving is the time for enjoying the ritual of feast and family assembly. It is a time for counting our blessings and good fortunes. We, in the organization, may wish to add thanks for the privilege of giving service—perhaps one of the greatest privileges of all. Our organization tries to serve the aged, the ill, the needy. We should also add thanks that our forefathers patterned a community to serve the spiritual and material needs of a diverse people. We should give thanks that ours is a land where people can still laugh, and dream, and hope, and speak our minds and worship as we please. We have much to be thankful for.

17. Speeches for Special Occasions

This chapter deals with speeches to stimulate a group of people. The typical situations requiring such speeches are anniversary memorials, dedications, commencement exercises and the like. On these occasions there is the opportunity to recall the traditions and ideals—patriotic, religious and social—and to deepen the reverence and enthusiasm of the audience for the lives and principles of great men.

The examples given in this chapter by no means cover all the situations in which speeches to stimulate and inspire are appropriate. The illustrations given are:

> Birthday of a great person
> Commencement
> Memorial Ceremonies
> Dedication of Home for Aged
> Dedication of Plaque
> Friendship
> Greetings to Forum

Illustration 1 — Birthday of a great person

Yesterday passed quietly here in our wonderful country. Few took time to remember, but it was the birthday of a great American—Franklin Delano Roosevelt. As we think back on his life we realize the importance to all mankind of freedom from want, and freedom from fear, that he fought for so valiantly. He was stricken down fighting for mankind; he was literally killed on the battle-field of freedom. Today, freedom of speech, freedom of religion, freedom from want, and freedom from fear are further from reality than at any time during peace. Whether we have these great freedoms depends on Americans—it depends on whether we keep them inviolate here and let them extend throughout the world. The very thinking that these freedoms inspire destroys prejudice, promotes brotherhood, insures peace, and brings a glimmer of sunlight into the souls of men.

Illustration 2 — Commencement

To receive a degree from this school is an honor which is especially welcome to anyone who entertains—as I do —a profound and abiding faith in our American way of life. Here in Main School you believe in freedom of enterprise and you are dedicated to the proposition that individual success and social responsibility can and should go together. Perhaps that is why the contribution which this small school has made to good citizenship has been out of proportion to its size. Its alumni have achieves some of the highest positions of leadership in business and in the professions. That is a record of which you may well be proud and it explains why I am so happy to receive your invitation to participate in these commencement day exercises.

I am fully aware, however, that anyone who accepts such an invitation has a delicate task to perform. His first duty, of course, is to congratulate the members of the graduating class. For all of you it is my sincere wish that you will find in your business and professional lives a source of great joy and happiness. Today you become part of the world at a time when it is seriously disturbed. Never in our history has there been a greater need for wise, courageous and enlightened leadership than at the present. It is to you, and young men and women like you, that we must look for that leadership. May God speed you. May you find an interesting and satisfying lifework in a world at peace.

Illustration 3 — Memorial Ceremonies

I ask you to please rise for a few moments of silence out of respect to the memory of a man who was with us yesterday, serving with us the needs of the community. My heart is full, full of sadness, and at the same time full of gratitude that it was my privilege, as it was yours, to be associated with him in the work to which he had dedicated himself and to which you are dedicated.

John Jones was not only a devoted and loyal community worker but was much more. He was a good man. A man of integrity, of deep sincerity. He loved his fellowman. No one could help being at ease in his presence. It was his idea to make those around him feel he was their friend. His features instantly impressed one with their kindly expression, and with a warm handshake or a gentle touch on the shoulder he could win the heart of anyone he met. He gave himself to the work in which we are dedicated. He believed as we believe. He felt as we do. He shared with us our ideals, our thoughts and principles, our desires, and our dedicated service.

Now he has passed on. It is with a sad heart and a tearful eye that we prepare for the final farewell. I am sure, if anyone deserved a reward beyond this mundane world, John Jones deserves it fully. He earned it because of his services to his fellowmen in this world.

Illustration 4 — Dedication of Home for Aged

I congratulate the community upon the finishing, the perfecting, the forging of this appropriate and efficient Home for the Aged. The care of our aged is the holiest of all of our obligations. The obligation applies to us all individually and collectively. Our elders must be kept healthy and happy and we should not rely on government alone to take care of them. It is not only a real joy to be able to take care of those who have cared for us and brought us to this time of our lives but it is our responsibility. The average age to which people live has increased. When we live so long some of our later years are spent in declining health and strength. It is hard to dress and get about. We need a little help and later on a little more. Finally a steadying hand is not enough and the wheel chair comes. Many of our people in the seventies and eighties are up and about until the last day of life.

In an infirmary, while getting the help and kindness needed, life becomes pleasant to them to its end. On this day we accept with utmost gratitude and dedicate the Home for the Aged. I wish publicly to express my sincere thanks to the great many people who aided in bringing about the completion of this great work. I owe my thanks to the other members of the board for their very fine coöperation. I owe sincere thanks to our village president who aided me materially in this work. I owe thanks to a great many other men and women who by their contributions made possible this magnificent event.

Illustration 5 — Dedication of Plaque

This organization, for many years, has set aside a day in honor of our departed members. In doing so we are carrying on one of the many high traditions of which we are proud. We pause momentarily to reflect on the many noble deeds of our departed brothers. They helped establish the glorious history of this organization. We today are reaping the rewards of their steadfast loyalty to the principles of the organization and the many sacrifices they made. It is up to us who are here today to see that this great organization for which they laid the foundation perpetuates the good work begun by them.

Today we are assembled here for still another purpose.

That purpose is to erect a perpetual testimonial to the memory of the ten gallant and courageous members of our order who gave their lives to safeguard the principles for which our nation went to war. We dedicate this plaque as a reminder to our present members. I therefore unveil this plaque to their honored memory and the preservation of their patriotic ideals.

Illustration 6 — Friendship

In our lobby is a sign which reads: "The Spirit of Our Club: Under this roof you need no formal introduction. Speak to others as you would have them speak to you and do it first." We want to make this a friendlier environment. The art of making friends is simply to be a friend. To have friends you must be friendly. Many a man wants to extend his hand, wishes to say a cheery word of greeting, desires with all his heart to be "one of the fellows" but is too shy to do it. The root of personal shyness is the fear of being laughed at. No one will laugh at you here.

Friendliness begets friendliness. The man who is cordial will find hands springing out to meet his. He will learn that a genuine interest in a neighbor produces real interest in him. There is a simple formula for spreading the cement of friendship and brotherly love. It is composed of ten ingredients in about equal parts. Arranged in proper order, the first letters of this formula supplies a word which is the key to the whole mystery. I will let you discover the word for yourselves. The formula is frankness, responsiveness, idealism, enthusiasm, nobility of purpose, dependability, selflessness, harmony, industry and patience. And the word is—Friendship.

Illustration 7 — Greetings to Forum

It is my privilege to greet you and to extend a warm welcome to our Civil Liberties Institute. One of the fundamental principles upon which the Institute was founded is that people should be free to develop their faculties. We believe liberty to be the secret of happiness and courage to be the secret of liberty. We believe that freedom to think as you will and to speak as you think are indispensable to the discovery and spread of political truth; that without free speech and assembly, discussion would be futile; that with free speech and assembly, discussion affords protection against the spread of noxious doctrine. We believe that the greatest menace to freedom is an inert people; that public discussion is a political duty; that it is hazardous to discourage thought, hope and imagination; that fear breeds repression; that repression breeds hate; that hate menaces stable government. The Civil Liberties Institute hopes to make some contribution toward implementing these beliefs. We take encouragement and inspiration from your presence here and do indeed bid you welcome!

18. Speeches of Tribute to Deceased; Messages of Sympathy and Condolence; Notices and Announcements of Death

The tribute to one who has passed on, as well as the expression of sympathy and condolence or the announcement for publication, is a statement of (1) shock and sorrow, (2) praise or eulogy, and (3) sympathy and comfort for the family of deceased.

Following are expressions of the three elements which comprise the speech of tribute in which the speaker will recall to the minds of his listeners the virtues and qualities of one who is no longer with them. The illustrations which succeed these component parts are complete speeches of tribute.

The material and ideas presented may be used in composing written messages of sympathy and condolence and also announcements for publication in newspapers and periodicals. When brevity is necessary, as in a telegram, not all the characteristics described need be given.

1. Shock and sorrow

Again, with unexpected suddenness, death has come among us. John Jones has silently closed the door of life and departed from us never again to return. The shock of his death is visibly and profoundly felt by those with whom he had daily contact.

✦

It is with deepest regret that I announce the death of our friend, John Jones. I was grieved beyond measure to learn that death has removed him from our midst.

✦

Sorrow fills our hearts at this sad moment, a sorrow that is deep and personal. The news of the untimely death of John Jones came as a great shock. His departure was sudden, unexpected and particularly distressing.

✦

I wish to pause sadly to announce the passing of a very conscientious officer of our organization. The shocking news of his death has just reached me.

✦

The very sad tidings that Sam Jones had passed to his eternal reward came to my attention late yesterday. His passing was quite sudden.

✦

I was saddened by the news of the death of your devoted husband who was my faithful friend. My heart is heavy. His sudden passing was a great blow to those who knew him.

I could not hold back the tears when I read in the newspapers of the passing of my close friend.

✦

In the death of Joseph Lawton, the Bar mourns the loss of one of its able members.

✦

It is difficult indeed to find words to express our regret at the death of this splendid man.

✦

It is with profound grief that we learn that the inexorable laws of Fate has decreed that our good brother, John Jones, be taken from us and obliged to move through the Celestial Gate to enter that bourn from which no traveler returns.

✦

We interrupt the usual routine of the program to note the passing of a great public servant, an intimate friend and associate. We pause to pay our tribute of love and affection and respect to his memory.

✦

The lodge pauses to note on its minutes its great sorrow at the passing of Robert Smith who was a member for 25 years.

✦

We pause in our activities this evening to pay a richly deserved tribute to the memory of a devoted and highly esteemed officer of our lodge, Brother John Jones, who yesterday passed to his eternal reward.

2. Praise or eulogy

Despite his very active life in fraternal activities and the numerous demands upon his time, he was first and foremost a family man. He loved to be with his family. He was a devoted husband to his dear wife. He was an affectionate father to his children.

✦

The character of the life he lived might be summed up in a few words: he was sincere, he was earnest, he was loyal, he was industrious, he was self-sacrificing. I know no one in the fraternity who tried harder to interpret the wishes of the men he led and served.

✦

He was a splendid man, of great intellect and big heart. This loved and loving husband and father was also my friend and colleague through all the years when our work in the capitol brought us into daily association. It was my privilege to know him through most of the years he served as president of our organization. He combined with his charm an unlimited energy and the highest integrity. His genial personality and the generous instincts of this fine man will be missed not only by the officers but by everybody in the organization.

✦

My foremost thought at this moment is that the passing of so great a champion of civil liberties will be felt not only throughout the city but the nation.

✦

Our college will be a living monument to his foresight and his indefatigable devotion to youth, to education and to humanity. No one ever again will embody all his traits—his professional attainment, his courage, his dedication to service.

✦

In closing, I should like to paraphrase the words of the great Abraham Lincoln, who, in a memorable address, said: "The world will little note, nor long remember what we say here, but it can never forget what they did here." In this instance, Samuel Jones, an honored, respected, and revered member of our noble profession, gave of himself unstintingly to the preservation of human rights and liberties and was ever zealous to take and carry through to its ultimate conclusion the cause of those who needed sound, experienced, and wise counsel.

✦

Here was a man of superlatively high standards, complete integrity, and boundless enthusiasm for whatever task he took in hand. No one, whose privilege it was to know him, is likely to forget the candor of his speech, the courage of his faith, the warm and glowing brightness of his friendship. He never dodged a responsibility, never refused to take on a hard job if it needed to be done. What he preached, he practiced. What he believed, he believed with heart and soul. He fought hard for every cause in which he enlisted, and the causes for which he fought were good and right.

✦

He was a quiet, perhaps overly modest man, inclined to be extremely cautious in his personal relationships, acutely conscious of his responsibilities and prone to deprecate his own charms and abilities.

He verily and truly exemplified the spirit of our fraternity: "To help the needy, to succor the distressed, and support everything that is fine and noble."

✦

Her life was the epitome of courage, vision and deep faith—an example worthy of emulation by all who love their fellowmen.

✦

He held positions of trust and died in the full tide of a career which gave great promise of future usefulness.

✦

He was much esteemed in the community in which he lived and was generally recognized as one whose acts and deeds were worthy of emulation.

✦

To all of us in the industry he was and always will be an ideal. The example he set will long continue to influence and inspire us.

✦

We found him at all times a man of understanding, sympathy, learning and integrity.

✦

His untarnished life leaves with us an example and inspiration for higher and nobler deeds.

3. Sympathy and comfort

I extend to you my deepest sympathy.

✦.

There is little I can say that will comfort you in this hour of your bereavement.

Please accept for yourself, and all who mourn with you, our assurance of heartfelt sympathy.

◆

I, his many friends, and the community will miss him. His passing grieves me inexpressibly.

◆

No one can better appreciate than I, who am myself utterly heartbroken by the loss of my own beloved husband, what your suffering must be and I pray you may be supported by Him to Whom alone the sorely stricken can look for comfort in this hour of heavy affliction.

◆

All of us in the fraternity have suffered a heavy loss in his death.

◆

We feel a keen sense of loss in his passing. It is difficult adequately to express our grief.

◆

God bless you and keep you in this your hour of sorrow.

◆

We all felt his severe loss very deeply, but some small measure of consolation may be found in the words of the poet, Walt Whitman:

> He is not gone. He is just away,
> With a cheery smile and the wave of the hand,
> He has wandered into an unknown land,
> And left us wondering how very fair that land
> May be, since he tarries there.

May the bereaved family find solace in the inspiring memories of the exemplary life of the departed.

✦

We are all comforted in the knowledge that he lives in the minds and hearts of everyone. God bless you and keep you in your hour of sorrow.

✦

We join in extending to the members of his bereaved family our heartfelt sympathy and pray that in the years that lie ahead the good Lord will sustain them and give them peace and health.

✦

May his soul rest in everlasting peace and may the Almighty grant solace and consolation to his dearly beloved wife and the members of his grief-stricken family.

✦

His passing leaves a void in our hearts and in the organization that will be difficult to fill. It is with the deepest sorrow and the deepest grief that we learn of his passing.

✦

Words are futile at a time like this to assuage the anguish of his family or of his friends. We can only bow our heads to the will of God, the Father of us all, and say to ourselves:

Is there beyond the silent night an endless day?
Is death a door that leads to light?
We cannot say.

The tongueless secret locked in fate
We cannot know.
We watch and wait.

◆

May he enjoy his eternal rest and the rewards he has earned.

◆

May her family derive some measure of comfort in the knowledge that we share their grief with them.

Illustration 1

We meet tonight under the shadow of a great loss in the passing of our beloved secretary, John Doe. Though the certainty of death and the uncertainty of life is ever with us, each visit of the Grim Reaper brings new sorrow and humbles us in our mad struggle for glory and fulfillment of ambition. Once again, necessarily, we should pause to reflect and consider the life and the work of our friend, and from his achievements seek to gain inspiration and courage to meet the trials and the tribulations of ordinary mortal existence. As a leader of the community, and a man, he built a temple of honor and of virtue, of industry and of unselfish devotion to duty. To the members of the bereaved family we extend our profound condolences, drawing consolation in the fullness of his life's services to his fellowmen.

Illustration 2

Our secretary, John Doe, has been taken from us. Sorrow fills our hearts at this sad moment, a sorrow that is deep and personal. The news of his untimely death came as a great shock. The simplicity and sweetness of his character have endeared him to us. In his passing I feel a personal loss too great to put into words. May his soul rest in everlasting peace, and may the Almighty grant solace and consolation to his dearly beloved wife and the members of his grief-stricken family.

Illustration 3

The sudden passing of John Doe was a great shock to those who knew him. He was fair, sympathetic, and always sought to do his duty honorably and justly. I can only add to what has already been said, that his loss is one which it will be difficult to overcome.

Illustration 4

It becomes our distressing duty to take notice of the death on Friday of John Doe, whose years of service were distinguished by his integrity and devotion to duty. By his death, his colleagues will miss a rare friendliness and charm of personality; this lodge will be deprived of the services of a valuable officer; and the fraternity will lose a faithful friend.

Illustration 5

It is impossible to speak of John Doe other than in superlatives. Loveable, gentlemanly, scholarly, kindly—

he was a man in the very best sense of that meaningful
term. Those who knew him loved him; the better they
knew him the more they loved him. He possessed great
personal charm; men were drawn to him irresistibly. John
Doe now rests in peace, but his noble and resplendent
spirit remains to comfort us. He is deep in our hearts,
and will continue there, warmly, as long as there is life
within us. His sterling qualities and his great works
live on.

Illustration 6

In the passing of John Doe I have lost a great and good
friend, whose encouragement, counsel and wisdom have
meant so much to me over the years. The cause of charity
has lost a leader who gave unstintingly of his labor and
his time. We shall all miss him. His passing is a great
blow to his colleagues on the Board, where intimacy of
association added love to the respect entertained for him.

Illustration 7

It was my good fortune to meet John Doe a few years
ago. My contacts with him were frequent. He radiated
from his personality a charm and sweetness. As we go
through this busy life, each striving selfishly to survive,
becoming callous to the sufferings of our fellows, it is
remarkable and unique to meet a personality like that of
John Doe. I know that the impress he left upon me was
a durable one. I found him to be one of nature's own

noblemen. He touched nothing that he didn't brighten and better. I don't think there is any man who came in contact with him who didn't add to his own determination to be better and more sympathetic and generous to his fellowman. His passing leaves a void in our hearts and in the organization that will be difficult to fill. It is with the deepest sorrow and grief that we conclude this tribute.

Illustration 8

We come together this morning to pay tribute to the memory of one of our members and brothers, John Doe, who has passed through the valley of the shadow of death from which no one ever returns. He was a loveable soul. We, his brothers, who admired him and loved him so much, simplify this ceremony in an expression that has never left my mind. It speaks volumes: "You never lose what you love if you love what you lose."

Illustration 9

Only today I learned your sad news and my heart is with you. I know you are grateful that your father knew no protracted suffering and that he enjoyed a long and full life. Some men ask for death in one way. Some would prefer it in another. John Jones found death in the midst of the discharge of his duties. Also, you have the comfort of knowing that the devotion shown him by you and his other children enriched his later years. Withal, the loss of a parent is a sad thing and hard to bear. I only wish I knew of some way to help you through this heartbreaking time. I can only hope, that from now on, life will bring you only happy things.

Illustration 10

Let us pause to note that death has struck again. Death has removed from our midst Brother John Doe, a gifted and erudite newspaperman. In his passing, journalism has lost one of the leading editorial writers of this era. His was a career of incredible vigor and forcefulness. He was a relentless crusader for what he believed right. His claim to fame is secure. Sometimes we differed with him politically, but we recognized that he was a genius in his field. He left an indelible imprint on American journalism and the life of this nation. We feel a keen sense of loss in his passing.

Illustration 11

The untimely death of your son, Robert, has been a tragic loss. While no one can fully share the sorrow which the death of a loved one brings, he will be sorely missed by his friends, too. There should be some measure of consolation in knowing that he met death pridefully and manfully in the service of his country. May God bless you and keep you in this hour of sorrow.

Illustration 12

The shocking news of the tragic death of my colleague has just reached me. He was my warm personal friend. His passing grieves me inexpressibly.

Illustration 13

It is a shock to realize that John Doe, who was so good and so gifted, has passed to the Great Beyond. It is with a full heart that I offer you my deepest sympathy.

Illustration 14

I was saddened to learn of the sudden death of John Doe. I wish to convey to you and to the other members of your organization my deep sympathy upon the loss of this remarkable man. It was my privilege to know him through most of the years he served as president of your organization. He was a combination of unlimited energy and highest devotion. All of us in the fraternity have suffered a great loss.

Illustration 15

Though death has removed from our midst our beloved secretary, Harry Horn, his spirit and influence will abide with us and his example will be with us for many years. Our deepest sympathy to you and your family.

Illustration 16

The Community Council deeply regrets the death and feels the loss of the Reverend Father Donald Dolan, the great servant of the Lord in the church life of our community. He was the distinguished friend of all the community, regardless of race, or creed, whom he valiantly supported in their difficult times. They are grateful to him and devoutly bless his memory.

Illustration 17

The officers, Executive Board, and members of the Community Center sorrowfully announce the death of our president, John Doe, who for many years devoted himself unselfishly to the interests of the Center. His friendly and kindly spirit will be greatly missed by all of us who had the privilege of serving with him. Because of his interest in humanitarian endeavors, his loss will be deeply felt by a great many.

Illustration 18

The officers of The Welfare Fund wish to express their grief over the untimely death of Mrs. Mary Roe, who served as chairman of our Executive Board. She gave unstintingly of herself as a leader of women and devoted her life to the cause of philanthropy. The example of her courage will remain as a source of continued inspiration to all of us. To her family and many friends we extend our heartfelt sympathy.

Illustration 19

The founder of our organization, John Doe, our inspiring leader, was identified for 25 years with the struggle for decency, justice and security. He devoted to the cause of labor and to his country a sincerity of purpose and intelligence of outlook which are the hallmark of a great man. His passing removes from the scene a peerless partisan of labor who fought a good fight for trade unionists everywhere, and a dauntless citizen who persevered to achieve a better and more secure America in a better and more secure world. He will be mourned long and sincerely, not only by working men and women throughout the world, but by all who aspire to a better way of life.

Illustration 20

The lodge pauses to note its great sorrow at the passing of Brother John Doe who served as our president for twelve years. Brother Doe had been ill for some time, but he insisted on performing his lodge duties whenever he felt physically able to come to meetings. It was that devotion to duty which brought about several heart attacks culminating in his death. His untimely death at age 60 is probably the result of the tremendous force and energy which he had put into the various offices which he had graced.

John Doe, in his years of efficient service to the lodge and in the high quality of his work as secretary, has merited the commendation of his brothers. The officers and members on this occasion join in paying this tribute to a good and faithful brother. He lives in our memory as a kindly soul who helped his fellowman. May God rest his soul!

Illustration 21

No one has served the Church with more devotion or with such fearless courage as the Reverend Father John Jones. He was a champion of all causes he believed to be right. As a churchman and as a citizen he rendered faithful service. He will be long remembered for his many contributions to the life of our community. Not the least of these is the part he played in the development of the movement for slum clearance and his courageous support of racial justice. We pray the Almighty God may grant him eternal rest.

19. Hints for Effective Speaking

Preliminary Considerations

An effective speech is one in which the speaker accomplishes his purpose of communicating ideas to an audience in a manner pleasing to them. The speaker should strive to make a good first impression. As he walks to the platform, greets his audience, utters his first sentences, his listeners are forming their first impression. He must, in the first few minutes, win the audience's approval of him, his subject matter and its development. He must appear confident, relaxed, and enthusiastic. He must never communicate any apprehension to his hearers. Of course, he must be sincere. There must be honesty in composition as well as in delivery if the speaker is to win over his audience.

Preparation is the best known guaranty against a poor performance. Its lack is the most common cause of stage fright. A contractor would not build a house without a blueprint and a speaker should not venture onto the platform unless he has prepared and practiced his talk. The preparation ought to begin long in advance of the speaking date and the work on the speech should be frequent. It is hard to force the development of a talk; speeches grow and should be given time to ripen.

When a speech has been carefully prepared, the

speaker can face his audience with confidence and assurance that his purpose will be attained.

The actual method of preparation varies with the speaker. Some write out their speeches word for word and then commit the entire speech to memory. Too often the memorized speech results in a stilted, inflexible presentation. Others think through their ideas carefully, writing down only the barest skeleton of an outline. The best course is carefully to plan the speech and to outline it in detail. Writing out a complete draft is helpful but the wording should not be committed to memory. The speaker should practice his speech out loud, choosing his words each time as he goes along.

By practicing a variety of words the speaker will develop a flexibility of expression. The outline should be used to fix firmly in mind the sequence of ideas. With practice the gist and order of the speech will be impressed upon his mind.

As the speaker practices he may feel impelled at various points to gesture and to emphasize certain words and thoughts. Gestures and emphasis so added are all to the good. The value of gestures is that they assist in the communication of ideas, help to hold the audience's attention and serve as an outlet for the speaker's tension, thereby increasing his self-confidence.

To help make a good impression, the speaker should look directly at his hearers. Just as he would do in speaking to a group of three or four, he will turn from one member of the audience to another taking in as many as he can. The speaker must convey the impression that he is talking to his audience individually and not gazing over their heads. The audience want to feel a sense of personal relationship as if the speaker were engaging them in a conversation. Nothing is quite so important a means of establishing personal contact with the audience as the simple device of looking them in the eye.

The speaker, once on the platform, acknowledges the chairman with a pleasant nod or says, "Mr. Chairman," and faces the audience. Then he greets the audience with a smile. Under proper circumstances, his salutation to the audience might be, "Fellow members of the Literary Society," or "Ladies and gentlemen." Then he is ready to begin.

In his opening sentences, to win the confidence and good will of his hearers, he should say something pleasant and agreeable. The guest-of-honor at an installation ceremony in response to expressions of tribute said:

Illustration 1

It is not easy to tell you of the happiness which your presence brings to an already full heart. I shall long remember the sacrifice which you made to come here to greet me. I earnestly hope that this ceremony was not a trespass upon your time and patience.

The effect of such a beginning, sincerely spoken, would tend to commend him to the audience's goodwill and kindness.

The Central or Main Idea

Getting across to the audience the central theme or idea is a matter that overshadows practically all else.

Clear organization of the speech is the first essential. If the speaker is making his point in an earnest and enthusiastic way, the audience will not only listen but will overlook many faults in form. The speaker should use specific data and examples of the point he is trying to make. He must be precise. An audience is not likely to accept vaguely expressed ideas. Many of the illustrations given in this book are purposely bare and unadorned. They are thought skeletons, but it is the meat which the speaker puts on that skeleton that will give them body, warmth and reality for the audience.

If, for instance, the speaker is delivering a speech of tribute at a testimonial dinner, the central idea is that the guest-of-honor is a deserving person. Uttering mere platitudes would not impress. The speaker should tell why the guest-of-honor is a deserving person and support the conclusion with facts.

Illustration 2

Robert Roe added strength and stature to the organization when he assumed the presidency. As a result of his forward-looking policies, our membership has doubled in the four years he has been at the helm and our organization has become a powerful force. He accepted what is essentially a thankless job holding no reward but the opportunity to serve. To perform the duties of president Robert Roe has taken time out from a lucrative business and his service to us has been at a tremendous personal sacrifice. He has been a most capable administrator. He succeeded in coördinating the functions of all sections of our order so that they now work together as one cohesive unit. He has stressed competence and good organization. He is not one to make hasty decisions. But once after study and investigation he reached a decision, it was forcefully executed.

He has a long and active record of civic participation and holds a high place in the community. Last year he was chosen to head the drive for the Hospital Fund and the results of his efforts were most gratifying. We can feel a deep and lasting satisfaction in having him as our president. He served us well. His excellent record deserves generous recognition.

If the object of the speech is to inform, the main purpose is to increase the audience's store of knowledge. To do this effectively the speaker must present enough concrete examples and precise information to avoid becoming vague and dry.

The following excerpt from President Eisenhower's State-of-the-Union message to Congress (Jan. 6, 1955) illustrates the speech to inform:

Illustration 3

I believe it would be well to remind ourselves of this great fundamental in our national life: our common belief that every human being is divinely endowed with dignity and worth and inalienable rights. This faith, with its corollary—that to grow and flourish people must be free—shapes the interests and aspirations of every American.

From this deep faith have evolved three main purposes

of our Federal government: First, to maintain justice and freedom among ourselves and, to champion them for others so that we may work effectively for enduring peace; second, to help keep our economy vigorous and expanding, thus sustaining our international strength and assuring better jobs, better living, better opportunities for every citizen; and third, to concern ourselves with the human problems of our people so that every American may have the opportunity to lead a healthy, productive and rewarding life. Foremost among these broad purposes of government is our support of freedom, justice and peace.

THE CONCLUSION

It was indicated that the first impression is a prime concern of the speaker, but the last impression is also important. Many a speech well begun has ended disastrously because of a poor conclusion. Last impressions often erase from memory impressions made earlier. The speaker dare not neglect the conclusion. This is his last opportunity to stress his main ideas. He should permit no one in the audience to leave with any doubt as to what he is trying to say. In the closing sentences, if the speech is to gain action, the speaker will ask the audience to do something, to contribute to some worthy cause, or to participate in some activity.

Illustration 4

I ask you, therefore, not to go away simply feeling satisfied and proud of the national candidates your party has chosen. There is something else to be done and it is up to you to do it. I urge you not to overlook the need to elect the right men to local and state offices. I believe most deeply that the roots of good government in this country lie in clean, honest and efficient local and state government. Many citizens are concerned with electing able, honest men to national office, but, I am afraid they overlook dishonesty and incompetence in their own back yards. We want clean, efficient government in this country from the towns and cities all the way up the ladder to Washington. And the only way to get it is to vote for the right men on election day.

If the object of the speech is one to inform as, for example, a demonstration of the greatness of our Constitution, a sample of the speaker's conclusion follows:

Illustration 5

Be grateful, therefore, for your heritage. Be proud and happy for the benefits the Constitution confers and pray God for a continuance of those benefits.

The ultimate value of training in effective speech will depend upon what the reader does with his knowledge of the principles given here. Skill in speaking grows weaker with disuse; but it develops strength from constant practice. The reader should participate to the fullest extent in the programs and meetings of the organizations to which he belongs. Only by constantly applying the principles studied will they remain fresh in mind and the effectiveness of his delivery will then keep pace with his growing knowledge.

Index